THE
LUCENT
TERRORISM
LIBRARY

Civil Liberties
and the
War on Terrorism

James D. Torr

LUCENT
BOOKS®

THOMSON

™

GALE

San Diego • Detroit • New York • San Francisco • Cleveland • New Haven, Conn. • Waterville, Maine • London • Munich

For more information, contact
Lucent Books
27500 Drake Rd.
Farmington Hills, MI 48331-3535
Or you can visit our Internet site at http://www.gale.com

LIBRARY OF CONGRESS CATALOGING-IN-PUBLICATION DATA

Torr, James D., 1974–
  Civil liberties and the war on terrorism / by James D. Torr.
    p. cm. — (Lucent terrorism library series)
  Includes bibliographical references.
  ISBN 1-59018-527-7
  1. Civil rights—United States—Juvenile literature. 2. Terrorism—United States—Prevention—Juvenile literature. 3. War on Terrorism, 2001—Juvenile literature.
  I. Title. II. Series: Lucent terrorism library.
  JC599.U5T66 2004
  323'.0973—dc22
                                                                2004000389

Contents

Foreword

It was the bloodiest day in American history since the battle of Antietam during the Civil War—a day in which everything about the nation would change forever. People, when speaking of the country, would henceforth specify "before September 11" or "after September 11." It was as if, on that Tuesday morning, the borders had suddenly shifted to include Canada and Mexico, or as if the official language of the United States had changed. The difference between "before" and "after" was that pronounced.

That Tuesday morning, September 11, 2001, was the day that Americans began to learn firsthand about terrorism, as first one fuel-heavy commercial airliner, and then a second, hit New York's World Trade Towers—sending them thundering to the ground in a firestorm of smoke and ash. A third airliner was flown into a wall of the Pentagon in Washington, D.C., and a fourth was apparently wrestled away from terrorists before it could be steered into another building. By the time the explosions and collapses had stopped and the fires had been extinguished, more than three thousand Americans had died.

Film clips and photographs showed the horror of that day. Trade Center workers could be seen leaping to their deaths from seventy, eighty, ninety floors up rather than endure the 1,000-degree temperatures within the towers. New Yorkers who had thought they were going to work were caught on film desperately racing the other way to escape the wall of dust and debris that rolled down the streets of lower Manhattan. Photographs showed badly burned Pentagon secretaries and frustrated rescue workers. Later pictures would show huge fire engines buried under the rubble.

It was not the first time America had been the target of terrorists. The same World Trade Center had been targeted in 1993 by Islamic terrorists, but the results had been negligible. The worst of such acts on American soil came in 1995 at the hands of a homegrown terrorist whose hatred for the government led to the bombing of the federal building in Oklahoma City. The blast killed 168 people—19 of them children.

But the September 11 attacks were far different. It was terror on a frighteningly well-planned, larger scale, carried out by nineteen men from the Middle East whose hatred of the United States drove them to the most appalling suicide mission the world had ever witnessed. As one U.S. intelligence officer told a CNN reporter, "These guys turned airplanes into weapons of mass destruction, landmarks familiar to all of us into mass graves."

Some observers say that September 11 may always be remembered as the date that the people of the United States finally came face to face with terrorism. "You've been relatively sheltered from terrorism," says an Israeli terrorism expert. "You hear about it happening here in the Middle East, in Northern Ireland, places far away from you. Now Americans have joined the real world where this ugliness is almost a daily occurrence."

This "real world" presents a formidable challenge to the United States and other nations. It is a world in which there are no rules, where modern terrorism is war not waged on soldiers, but on innocent people— including children. Terrorism is meant to shatter people's hope, to create instability in their daily lives, to make them feel vulnerable and frightened. People who continue to feel unsafe will demand that their leaders make concessions—*do something*— so that terrorists will stop the attacks.

Many experts feel that terrorism against the United States is just beginning. "The tragedy is that other groups, having seen [the success of the September 11 attacks] will think: why not do something else?" says Richard Murphy, former ambassador to Syria and Saudi Arabia. "This is the beginning of their war. There is a mentality at work here that the West is not prepared to understand."

Because terrorism is abhorrent to the vast majority of the nations on the planet, President George W. Bush's declaration of war against terrorism was supported by many other world leaders. He reminded citizens that it would be a long war, and one not easily won. However, as many agree, there is no choice; if terrorism is allowed to continue unchecked the world will never be safe.

The volumes of the Lucent Terrorism Library help to explain the unexplainable events of September 11, 2001, as well as examine the history, personalities, and issues connected with the ensuing war on terror. Annotated bibliographies provide readers with ideas for further research. Fully documented primary and secondary source quotations enliven the text. Each book in this series provides students with a wealth of information as well as launching points for further study and discussion.

Introduction

Liberty vs. Security: A Necessary Trade-Off?

President George W. Bush first proclaimed America's war on terrorism in a speech before Congress on September 20, 2001. In it, he outlined the steps that the U.S. government would take to apprehend terrorists and prevent further terrorist attacks. These steps include increased intelligence gathering abroad, an expansion of the role of the Federal Bureau of Investigation (FBI) in preventing terrorism at home, and the mobilization of the National Guard. "Many will be involved in the effort," he said, "from FBI agents to intelligence operatives to the reservists we have called to active duty."[1] And to coordinate the efforts of all the various federal agencies involved in counterterrorism, Bush announced the creation of a new federal Department of Homeland Security. In the following weeks, Bush made it clear that the U.S. government would play a much greater role then ever before in both investigating suspected terrorists and implementing security measures to protect Americans.

Americans certainly want the government to do more to prevent terrorism. But as many U.S. leaders have pointed out, there is danger in the government becoming too involved in the lives of its citizens. The United States, after all, was founded on the rights, also called civil liberties, of an individual to be free from unwarranted government interference. The Constitution's Bill of Rights enumerates several of these civil liberties—for example, freedom of speech, freedom of association, freedom from unwarranted searches, and the right to due process of law when charged with a crime. In prosecuting the war on terrorism, the United States is faced with a dilemma: Americans want to give the government the power it needs to prevent terrorism, but Americans also want to preserve their freedom from government control.

Security Without Liberty

To better understand the tension between liberty and security, consider how a society that does not value individual freedom might deal with terrorism. Unconstrained by concerns about its citizens' rights, the government of such a society could enact policies based solely on how effective they were at deterring terrorists.

The first step such a society might take would be to investigate suspected terrorists. Without any regard for suspects' rights, the government would be free to search suspects' homes at any time and monitor their private communications. The government might arrest and imprison suspects

After the September 11, 2001, terrorist attacks, President George W. Bush created the Department of Homeland Security to coordinate the efforts of federal agencies involved in the fight against terrorism.

without proof of guilt (perhaps staging trials to give the appearance of fairness), reasoning that it would be better to lock up a few innocent people than to let a single terrorist go free. It might employ torture in questioning suspects. Such a society, where law enforcement is valued more than freedom, is often referred to as a police state.

The government might also take control of the media in order to limit the effectiveness of terrorist attacks. If an attack occurred, the government would be able to downplay or even deny the incident altogether, thus reducing terrorists' ability to spread fear through violence.

The society might also try to suppress dissent, reasoning that if no one in the country is allowed to express controversial views, then it will be harder for would-be terrorists to recruit fellow conspirators. Individuals who belong to groups or religions that are openly critical of the government would be investigated and possibly arrested. The government might control what types of opinions and ideas are expressed in the media, censoring anything that could potentially incite anyone to violence or rebellion.

Because terrorists could still enter from outside the country, the government would likely limit immigration and track the movements of immigrants and citizens who have traveled outside the country. Individuals might be required to obtain government permission to leave the country or even to travel from one region to another within the country. These movement-tracking and -control systems would

be useless if people were able to pretend they were someone they were not, so the government would have to develop ways of validating people's identities, for example, through fingerprints or government-issued identification cards.

A government that does not value individual freedom simply has more options in fighting terrorism than a democratic society that does value civil liberties. For this reason, writes Harvard law professor Alan Dershowitz, "Terrorism is a tactic directed most effectively at open democracies. It is far less effective against closed tyrannies [that] can employ the most brutal countermeasures against terrorists, their supporters, their families, their co-religionists, and anyone else."[2] Dershowitz points to societies such as Iraq under former dictator Saddam Hussein and the former Soviet Union as examples of such tyrannies.

A Balancing Act?

As a democracy, the United States faces a more difficult challenge in dealing with terrorism: The purpose of a democracy is to defend the liberty of its citizens. The United States might better be able to defend the nation against terrorism if the government restricts some liberties—but should it?

The American public seems divided on this issue. In a poll taken just weeks after the September 11 attacks, *Newsweek* found that 63 percent of the public agreed that the average person would have to give up some civil liberties to fight terrorism. But almost a year later, in August 2002, only 47 percent agreed with the same statement, while 47

Benjamin Franklin believed in the importance of retaining individual liberties, even in the face of national danger.

percent disagreed. Other surveys have reported similar shifts in public opinion.

Many civil libertarians take an absolutist stance: They completely reject the idea that civil liberties should be curtailed because of terrorist threats. Benjamin Franklin captured this sentiment with a famous quote: "They that can give up essential liberty to obtain a little temporary safety deserve neither liberty nor safety."[3] After the September 11 attacks, Anthony Romero, executive director of the American Civil Liberties Union (ACLU), expressed Franklin's sentiment in different terms, asserting that to restrict liberty is to capitulate to terrorism:

The attack of September 11 not only targeted our personal lives and property, it was also an attack on freedom and equality that are the hallmarks of our democracy. Terror, by its very nature, is intended not only to destroy, but also to intimidate people, forcing them to take actions that are not in their best interest. That's why defending liberty in a time of crisis is the ultimate act of defiance. It's the ultimate act of patriotism. For, if we are intimidated to the point of restricting our freedoms, the terrorists will have won.[4]

For many civil libertarians, then, curtailments of civil liberties are simply not justified in the war on terrorism.

More often, however, the debate about liberty and security is framed in terms of a trade-off, or balancing act. As *USA Today* reporter Gene Stephens writes, "Public policy is always about trade-offs and compromise. . . . What Americans need is a comfortable balance between safety and freedom."[5] Those who support this view believe that increased protection from terrorism is worth some limited curtailments of civil liberties. Writing in the *Atlantic Monthly,* for example, law professor Richard Posner argues that, in the wake of September 11,

> it stands to reason that our civil liberties will be curtailed. They *should* be curtailed, to the extent that the benefits in greater security outweigh the costs in reduced liberty. All that can reasonably be asked of the responsible legislative and judicial officials is that they weigh the costs as carefully as the benefits.[6]

From this cost-benefit point of view, the United States may have to enact some minor curtailments on individual freedom in order protect Americans' core liberties.

The USA PATRIOT Act

In the aftermath of the September 11 attacks, the U.S. government generally adopted the cost-benefit point of view. A consensus emerged in Congress that the FBI and other law enforcement agencies needed expanded powers to meet the terrorist threat. The difficult choices, of course, were in the details—in the specific policies enacted. For example, of course the U.S. government would not abandon the Fourth Amendment's protection against unwarranted search and seizure, but might it be justified in making it easier for the FBI and other agencies to obtain search warrants in terrorism cases? And while the government should certainly preserve the Fifth Amendment's guarantee of due process under the law in criminal cases, might it be justified in detaining suspected terrorists even when the evidence for doing so is less than concrete?

These are some of the questions that Congress grappled with in the weeks after the September 11 attacks. While the FBI, Central Intelligence Agency (CIA), and other agencies were engaged in the largest criminal investigation in history—tracking down the al-Qaeda terrorists who helped plan the attacks—Attorney General John Ashcroft led the Bush administration's effort to persuade Congress to give new powers to these agencies. The result was the Uniting and Strengthening America by Providing Appropriate Tools Required to Intercept and Obstruct Terrorism Act of 2001—also known as the USA PATRIOT Act. The act was passed overwhelmingly in the House and almost unanimously in the Senate. President Bush signed the USA PATRIOT Act into law on October 26, 2001.

The USA PATRIOT Act gives government law enforcement and intelligence agencies a variety of new powers. First and foremost, the USA PATRIOT Act expands the definition of *terrorism* to include domestic, in addition to international, activities, and it gives law enforcement agencies much greater freedom to use wiretaps, monitor e-mail and Internet usage, access financial and medical records, and use other surveillance and investigation techniques on individuals suspected of domestic terrorism. The legislation also makes it easier for law enforcement officials to eavesdrop on communications between attorneys and their clients, and it authorizes the attorney general to detain noncitizen immigrants who are believed to pose a threat to national security.

Although the USA PATRIOT Act met with little congressional opposition, as America recovered from the September 11 attacks the USA PATRIOT Act became a source of increasing controversy. Critics of the act, such as the ACLU, contend that it "gives the Executive Branch sweeping new powers that undermine the Bill of Rights."[7] Supporters of the USA PATRIOT Act, such as Attorney General Ashcroft, maintain that the USA PATRIOT Act provides necessary law enforcement tools to win the war on terrorism. At one point Ashcroft openly criticized opponents of the act: "To those who scare peace-loving people with phantoms of lost liberty, my message is this: Your tactics only aid terrorists."[8] These competing claims illustrate the tension between security and freedom.

What Trade-Offs Are Justified?

Ultimately, the USA PATRIOT Act and other government counterterrorism measures put into place since September 11 have moved the debate beyond the issue of whether civil liberties should be curtailed and toward a discussion of which specific government policies are justified. As constitutional law expert Erwin Chemerinsky said a few weeks before the USA PATRIOT Act was passed, "It is so important for the debate to get past the point where one side is saying, 'We've got to give up civil liberties,' and the other side is saying, 'We cannot give up civil liberties.' . . . It has to be a much more nuanced discussion of what civil liberties are being compromised, under which circumstances, and for what gain."[9]

Evaluating the effectiveness of counterterrorism measures, however, can be difficult. Absent another terrorist attack, it may be impossible to prove whether a particular security measure has been successful or merely superfluous. In contrast, the impact that such measures have on individual freedom is often readily apparent. Airline travelers, for example, have certainly noticed the random baggage searches and other security checks that were quickly instituted at airports around the country.

The ACLU's Anthony Romero sums up civil libertarians' main criticism of the government's security measures: "So many of the efforts undertaken by the government are either not necessary or the tradeoff is wrong," [10] he says. The ACLU and other groups have taken action against a variety of these security measures. For example, several groups filed lawsuits asserting that the government was legally obligated to divulge the names of the immigrants detained in its terrorism investigations, and in August 2002 a federal judge ruled in the groups' favor. Other organizations, such as the Lawyers Committee for Human Rights (LCHR), have also filed legal briefs in lawsuits alleging that it is unconstitutional for the government to detain U.S. citizens without charge. Yet another group, the Electronic Privacy Information Center, has filed lawsuits against the government asserting that its secrecy measures in the war on terrorism violate the Freedom of Information Act. Finally, more than 140 cities and counties, in addition to state legislatures in Alaska,

Counterterrorist specialists, like these agents at CIA headquarters in Langley, Virginia, closely monitor the activities of suspected terrorists.

Hawaii, and Vermont, have approved resolutions condemning the USA PATRIOT Act and, in a few cases, refusing to enforce it.

In the face of this mounting criticism, in August 2003 Attorney General Ashcroft embarked on a speaking tour to defend the government's counterterrorism measures. "If we knew then what we know," said Ashcroft, "we would have passed the Patriot Act six months before September 11th rather than six weeks after the attacks. For Congress to have done less would have been a failure of government's most basic responsibility . . . to preserve life and liberty."[11] Ashcroft has also voiced support for the Domestic Security Enhancement Act—nicknamed "PATRIOT II"—which, if passed into law, would give further power to law enforcement agencies, including the authority to secretly arrest terrorism suspects.

Searching for Common Ground

While civil liberties groups continue to oppose the USA PATRIOT Act and other government initiatives, they acknowledge the need for increased security. The LCHR, for example, states, "We support efforts by the government to take appropriate measures to enhance public security, to gather information about potential attacks, to bring perpetrators of these crimes to justice, and to take precautionary steps to prevent future attacks."[12] But civil libertarians believe that these goals can be accomplished without curtailing freedoms. David Cole and James X. Dempsey, authors of *Terrorism and the Constitution,* write, "There is no necessary contradiction between a robust application of constitutional rights and an effective counterterrorism strategy."[13] In other words, as the ACLU puts it, "We can be both safe and free."[14]

Likewise, proponents of the government's security measures insist that their goal is to protect liberty, not curtail it. "Security is the means by which we ensure our fundamental freedoms," says former assistant attorney general Viet Dinh: "It is especially in this war, where our enemies are attacking the very foundation of our liberties, that we must be particularly vigilant in protecting those liberties."[15]

As the war on terrorism continues, so will the debate about restrictions on civil liberties. It may be, as many U.S. leaders believe, that the United States must strike the proper balance between security and freedom. Or it may be, as many civil libertarians argue, that the United States should look for ways to protect Americans without curtailing their liberties. As time goes on, hopefully civil libertarians and the officials leading the war on terrorism will be able to expand their common ground—they are, after all, each working to defend freedom.

Chapter One

A History of Civil Liberties During Wartime

History shows that curtailment of civil liberties—including the right to free speech, the right to a fair trial, and the right to equal protection under the law—has often followed national crises, particularly the outbreak of war. "Since the nation's founding, Americans have relied on basic legal protections spelled out by the Bill of Rights," writes reporter Angie Cannon, "but during past wartimes, civil liberties have been curbed dramatically."[16] From the Sedition Act of 1798—which made it a crime to criticize the government—to the internment of Japanese Americans during World War II, during times of crisis the United States has often curtailed civil liberties in ways that Americans later regretted. In waging the war on terrorism, one of the many challenges facing the United States is to avoid the civil liberties mistakes of the past.

The nation's founders, well aware of the tension between security and freedom, were concerned that Americans would be tempted to curtail civil liberties in times of war. In 1787, during the debates over the framing of the Constitution, Alexander Hamilton predicted that when faced with war or other threats, America would "resort for repose and security to institutions which have a tendency to destroy their civil and political rights. To be more safe, they, at length, become willing to run the risk of being less free."[17] In 1798, little more than a decade after the framing of the Constitution and only seven years after the Bill of Rights was ratified, Hamilton's fears were proved correct.

Free Speech and Sedition

In 1798 the French Revolution was still raging, and hostile French diplomatic actions had many Americans convinced that war with France was imminent. In addition, many French refugees had immigrated to the United States, and most of them supported the Republican Party, led by Thomas Jefferson. John Adams, a Federalist, was president at the time. The Federalists also controlled Congress and—partly because of hysteria over possible war with France, and partly to secure Federalist power against the Republicans—the legislature passed four laws. Known as the Alien and Sedition Acts, they targeted immigrants and made it a crime to criticize the government.

One of the four laws was the Naturalization Act, which postponed citizenship and voting privileges for immigrants from five years to fourteen years. Because many immigrants tended to vote Republican, this law greatly undermined the Republican Party. The Alien Act gave the president the power to deport aliens thought to present a danger to the government, and the Alien Enemies Act authorized the imprisonment and deportation of immigrants during wartime. Together, the alien acts foreshadowed the government's tendency to enact anti-immigrant measures in times of war.

The most controversial of the four laws, however, was the Sedition Act. The term *sedition* refers to the incitement of rebellion against a government, but the 1798 Sedition Act broadly prohibited all criticism of the government, outlawing "any false, scandalous and malicious writing or writings against the government of the United States, or either house of the

Congress of the United States, or the President of the United States." The broad terms of the law basically nullified the First Amendment's protection of free speech and freedom of the press. Prominent supporters of the Republican Party, many of them journalists, were arrested for criticizing the Federalists in power.

The Alien and Sedition Acts stand out as blotches on John Adams's presidency. As Ira Glasser, former executive director of the

Alexander Hamilton believed that the government would have to curtail the civil liberties of citizens in time of war.

The Sedition Act of World War I

Passed on May 16, 1918, the Sedition Act made it a crime to criticize the government or the war effort. An excerpt follows.

"Whoever, when the United States is at war, shall willfully make or convey false reports or false statements with intent to interfere with the operation or success of the military or naval forces of the United States, or to promote the success of its enemies, . . . and whoever, when the United States is at war, shall willfully cause or attempt to cause, or incite or attempt to incite, insubordination, disloyalty, mutiny, or refusal of duty, in the military or naval forces of the United States, or shall willfully obstruct or attempt to obstruct the recruiting or enlistment service of the United States, and whoever, when the United States is at war, shall willfully utter, print, write, or publish any disloyal, profane, scurrilous, or abusive language about the form of government of the United States, or the Constitution of the United States, or the military or naval forces of the United States, or the flag of the United States, or the uniform of the Army or Navy of the United States, or any language intended to bring the form of government of the United States, or the Constitution of the United States, or the military or naval forces of the United States, or the flag of the United States, or the uniform of the Army or Navy of the United States into contempt, scorn, contumely, or disrepute, or shall willfully utter, print, write, or publish any language intended to incite, provoke, or encourage resistance to the United States, or to promote the cause of its enemies, . . . and whoever shall willfully advocate, teach, defend, or suggest the doing of any of the acts or things in this section enumerated, and whoever shall by word or act support or favor the cause of any country with which the United States is at war or by word or act oppose the cause of the United States therein, shall be punished by a fine of not more than $10,000 or imprisonment for not more than twenty years, or both."

American Civil Liberties Union (ACLU), writes,

> The Alien and Sedition Acts identified no traitors and made no Americans safer. To the contrary, American citizens and their rights were the only casualties. The war with France never came, and the fear of the French subsided. No alien was ever deported or incarcerated, and a few years later the . . . residence requirement for citizenship reverted to five years. But the Sedition Act was widely enforced against American citizens, all of them . . . political opponents of President Adams and his administration's policies.[18]

All four of the laws were repealed or allowed to expire by 1802, and President Thomas Jefferson, elected in 1800, pardoned those imprisoned under the Sedition Act.

Yet more than a century later, the United States passed another Sedition Act, this time to suppress dissent against America's involvement in World War I. The

Sedition Act of 1918 made it a crime to "utter, print, write, or publish any disloyal, profane, scurrilous, or abusive language about the form of government of the United States" or to "encourage resistance to the United States." The act also authorized the postmaster general to seize mail that contained criticism of the government. U.S. leaders, concerned about the 1917 Bolshevik Revolution in Russia, a revolt of the working class, became particularly suspicious of Socialists and other left-wing groups. Eugene V. Debs, a labor leader, antiwar activist, and former Socialist Party candidate for president, was among the more than one thousand individuals imprisoned for violating the Sedition Act.

The Wisdom of Hindsight

In the second half of the twentieth century, the Supreme Court, over the course of several rulings, made it clear that both of the Sedition Acts had been unconstitutional. Today, the idea that Congress would pass a law abridging freedom of speech or freedom of the press is unthinkable to most Americans. In fact, defenders of the USA PATRIOT Act point out that although it expands the power of the FBI to search an individual's belongings and financial records, it only allows such searches if they are "not conducted solely upon the basis of activities protected by the first amendment to the Constitution."

However, the First Amendment only achieved its vaunted status after being so severely curtailed at two different points in U.S. history. As wrong as they may seem to modern Americans, the two sedition acts seemed justified to the leaders who enacted them and to many of the Americans who lived under them. As journalist Geoffrey R. Stone explains, "It is much easier to look back on past crises and find our predecessors wanting than it is to make wise judgments when we ourselves are in the eye of the storm. But that challenge now falls to us."[19]

Having been curtailed twice before, the right to criticize the government is now one of Americans' most cherished liberties. However, civil libertarians caution, the curtailment of other liberties that Americans take for granted—such as freedom from unwarranted search and seizure—may seem justified "in the eye of the storm," just as the Sedition Acts seemed justified to past generations. In addition, the war on terrorism is unlike conventional wars of the past: The security measures to combat terrorism are different than the measures used to fight traditional wars, and therefore the threats to civil liberties may be different as well.

Terrorist Bombings and the Palmer Raids

Compared to other countries, the United States does not have a great deal of experience in dealing with terrorist attacks on U.S. soil, but one incident stands out: the Palmer Raids of 1919 to 1921. In June 1919, the fighting in World War I had recently ended, but the United States was in political and economic turmoil. Workers had led the 1917 Bolshevik Revolution in

Russia, and many Americans were caught up in the "Red Scare," worrying that Russia's communism and political instability would take hold in the United States.

Amid this climate of social conflict, writes historian Bruce Watson, "the threat of terrorism sent Americans into a frenzy of fear." [20] A series of bombings and attempted bombings had begun on April 28, when a package of sulfuric acid and dynamite was mailed to Seattle's mayor. Then on the evening of June 2, bombs exploded in eight cities—in Washington, D.C., an Italian anarchist blew himself up outside the home of A. Mitchell Palmer, President Woodrow Wilson's attorney general. Palmer reacted to the bombings by ordering mass arrests of suspected Communists, Socialists, and anarchists. From June 1919 to early 1921, between six thousand and ten thousand people were arrested—five thousand of them in sweeping raids of thirty-three cities on January 2, 1920. Most of those arrested were noncitizen immigrants. Many were arrested solely because of their affiliation with a radical group, without warrants or evidence. More than two hundred immigrants were deported.

"Not for at least half a century," writes historian William Leuchtenberg, "had there been such a wholesale violation of civil liberties." [21] Palmer justified the raids by claiming that there was a terrorist conspiracy afoot. He predicted that there would be mass bombings on May 1, 1920. When none occurred, the Red Scare began to die down and a public backlash against the Palmer Raids began. The American Civil Liberties Union was founded in 1920 largely as a result of the civil liberties violations that occurred during the Palmer Raids. "The Palmer Raids trampled the Bill of Rights," states an ACLU pamphlet, "making arrests without warrants, conducting unreasonable searches and seizures, wantonly destroying property, using physical brutality against suspects, and detaining suspects without charges for prolonged periods. Palmer's men also invoked the wartime Espionage and Sedition Acts of 1917 and 1918 to deport noncitizens without trials." [22]

Targeting Immigrants

For civil libertarians, Attorney General John Ashcroft's ordering of mass arrests of immigrants after September 11 seemed like a frightening echo of the Palmer Raids. In the first few days after September 11, more than seven hundred foreigners were arrested and detained on immigration charges. Most were later released, but about one hundred were still being detained more than a year later. Civil libertarians argue that, as in the Palmer Raids, immigrants have become the primary targets of investigation, only now being Arab or Muslim has replaced being a Socialist or a Communist. The detainment of immigrants after September 11 also recalls the internment of Japanese Americans during World War II.

Following the Japanese surprise attack on Pearl Harbor, Hawaii, on December 7, 1941, millions of Americans feared that a Japanese invasion of the West Coast was imminent, and some members of the pub-

During World War II, the government relocated Japanese Americans to internment camps, such as this one in California.

lic and the military feared that the large numbers of Japanese immigrants and U.S.-born Japanese Americans living in California, Oregon, and Washington might aid such an invasion. President Franklin D. Roosevelt—who a few years earlier had declared, "If the fires of freedom and civil liberties burn low in other lands they must be made brighter in our own"[23]—gave in to the pressure to relocate Japanese Americans and immigrants away from the West Coast. In February 1942 Roosevelt signed an executive order authorizing the military to round up people of Japanese ancestry and forcibly relocate them to internment camps in eastern California and the Southwest. These people were forced to sell their homes, businesses, and farms at great losses and become prisoners for the duration of the war.

More than two-thirds of those relocated were American citizens, who were denied their constitutional rights to due process under the law and to equal treatment under the law. Yet, as Glasser of the ACLU notes, "Nearly all Americans accepted this, looked the other way, and felt safer because they were afraid."[24] Of course, the Japanese invasion of the West Coast never happened, and decades later, in 1988, Congress authorized monetary compensation for those who had been relocated and President Ronald Reagan issued a formal apology for the government's actions. During the actual crisis, though, the United States chose to try to increase safety at the expense of civil liberties.

Treatment of Persons Suspected of Criminal Activity

The sedition acts, the Palmer Raids, and the internment of Japanese Americans are just three of the most infamous violations of civil liberties during times of crises, in which the First Amendment and the rights of immigrants and minorities were clearly violated. At other points in history, the government has infringed on the right of individuals to be free from unwarranted searches and the right of those suspected

of a crime to defend themselves in a court of law.

During the Civil War, President Abraham Lincoln suspended the writ of habeus corpus, a constitutional provision that prohibits the government from detaining citizens without charge. The U.S. government's detention of thousands of terrorism suspects since September 11 has again raised questions about the suspension of the writ, and the Sixth Amendment's guarantee of a speedy and public trial, in times of crisis.

At the beginning of America's Cold War with the Soviet Union in the 1950s, Senator Joseph McCarthy and the House Un-American Activities Committee (HUAC) launched a hunt for Communist sympathizers and subversives. McCarthy's Senate committee and HUAC made sweeping accusations against individuals and organizations, often only on the evidence of unidentified informants. In show business, academia, and labor unions, many people's careers were ruined once they were labeled as Communist sympathizers by McCarthy or HUAC. Often people were identified as such based only on their ties to a left-wing organization. Some civil libertarians worry that the USA PATRIOT Act's harsh penalties for those with ties to terrorist organizations, and the way the USA PATRIOT Act defines the term "terrorist organization," could lead to charges of guilt by association as in the McCarthy era.

Finally, beginning in 1971, journalists and congressional investigation revealed that the U.S. government, through the Federal Bureau of Investigation (FBI), the

Central Intelligence Agency (CIA), and other agencies, had been spying on, and, in some cases, sabotaging the efforts of, civil rights and antiwar groups since the 1950s. The FBI and other law enforcement organizations used illegal wiretaps and other measures to monitor civil rights leaders such as Martin Luther King Jr., black-power groups such as the Black Panther Party, and a variety of organizations, including several independent newspapers,

that opposed the war in Vietnam. In the 1970s several steps were taken to limit intelligence organizations' authority to spy on U.S. citizens. As journalist Stuart Taylor Jr. explains,

> The Supreme Court, Congress, and the Ford and Carter administrations placed tight limits on law enforcement and intelligence agencies. The Court [restricted] government powers to

Overcoming Fear

The following excerpts are from a speech that Secretary of Transportation Norman Y. Mineta gave at the University of Rochester in 2001, in which he discussed his experience as a Japanese American during World War II and his hope that Americans will not react to the September 11 attacks with fear of and discrimination against minorities.

"As you know, more than a few journalists and historians have taken to describing September 11th as the new Pearl Harbor. The analogy is a good one—once again, the United States has been attacked without warning and without mercy. The attack has awakened us to a danger our Nation sometimes felt we would not have to face. And it has strengthened our resolve to face that danger—and remove it.

I think that all of you will understand that, as an American of Japanese ancestry, I find the analogy of Pearl Harbor to be particularly important. It highlights one of the greatest dangers that we will face as a coun-

try during this crisis—and that is, the danger that in looking for the enemy we may strike out against our own friends and neighbors. . . .

The internment of Japanese Americans during the Second World War has rightly been called the greatest mass abrogation of civil liberties in our Nation's history—and I believe that it stands as a warning to all of us of how dangerous misguided fear can be. . . .

We can resolve today, as Americans, that the tremendous progress we have made toward our goal of equal justice and equal opportunity for all Americans will not be sacrificed to fear.

The terrorists who committed the atrocities of September 11th . . . believe they can use the forces of terror and fear to make us fail our most basic principles, and to break our most sacred promises to each other. It is my greatest hope that, in the months and years ahead, all of us will join together as Americans to make sure they do not succeed."

search, seize, wiretap, interrogate, and detain suspected criminals (and terrorists). It also barred warrantless wiretaps and searches of domestic radicals. Congress barred warrantless wiretaps and searches of suspected foreign spies and terrorists—a previously untrammeled presidential power—in the 1978 Foreign Intelligence Surveillance Act. [25]

The USA PATRIOT Act, which removes some of these restrictions, has revived the debate about domestic intelligence programs and their potential for abuse.

Avoiding the Mistakes of the Past

Some proponents of the war on terrorism have downplayed America's history of curtailing civil liberties during wartime. Historian Jay Winik, for example, points out that although the United States has repeatedly curtailed civil liberties in times of crisis, it has also restored them once the crisis was past:

> Faced with the choice between security and civil liberties in times of crisis, previous presidents—John Adams, Abraham Lincoln, Woodrow Wilson and Franklin Roosevelt—to a man (and with little hesitation) chose to drastically curtail civil liberties. It is also worth noting that despite these previous and numerous extreme measures, there was little long-term or corrosive effect on society after the security threat subsided. When the crisis ended,

normalcy returned, and so too did civil liberties, invariably stronger than before. [26]

In addition, defenders of the USA PATRIOT Act and other measures in the war on terrorism argue that they are not nearly as drastic as civil liberties curtailments of the past.

Moreover, they argue that Americans will not repeat past mistakes. For example, Harvard law professor Laurence H. Tribe has applauded President Bush and other leaders for condemning discrimination against Muslims and Arab Americans. Discussing the anti-Japanese hysteria that followed the attack on Pearl Harbor, Tribe remarked, "How different was the sight of New York's Mayor Rudolph Giuliani, soon followed by President Bush, appealing eloquently to Americans not to seek revenge on their fellow citizens who happened to be Muslims." [27]

Civil libertarians insist, however, that upholding civil liberties in times of crisis requires constant vigilance. Again and again, they point out, when faced with a choice between security and civil liberties, Americans have chosen security. Although the nation as a whole has survived curtailments of civil liberties, countless individuals had constitutional rights violated by repressive laws and security measures. And often civil liberties have been curtailed unnecessarily, in the face of exaggerated threats. As journalist Daniel Hellinger writes, "Rather than defend the 'homeland' from terrorist attacks, abridgement of civil liberties has more often been aimed at suppressing

Lincoln's Suspension of the Writ of Habeus Corpus

One of the most well-known examples of the restriction of civil liberties during wartime is President Abraham Lincoln's suspension of the writ of habeus corpus during the Civil War. *Habeus corpus* is a Latin term which means "you should have the body," capturing the idea that the government should not detain people against their will without just cause. The Constitution guarantees that any person being held by the government has the right to request a writ of habeus corpus from the courts. If a court agrees to the request, then the government must demonstrate that it is holding the person in question for a compelling reason or else set the person free. The right to a writ of habeus corpus—essentially a guarantee against indefinite detention—is the only individual right to be included in the text of the original Constitution.

The Constitution states in Article 1, Section 9 that the writ may be suspended during national emergencies: "The privilege of the Writ of Habeas Corpus shall not be suspended, unless when in Cases of Rebellion or Invasion the public Safety may require it." Lincoln assumed this power to authorize the arrests and indefinite detention of thousands of Southern sympathizers. For generations, Civil War historians have argued over whether Lincoln's actions were justified and whether they were constitutional.

During the Civil War, Abraham Lincoln suspended the writ of habeus corpus in order to detain Confederate sympathizers without cause.

dissent, advancing some other agenda, or boosting the careers of unscrupulous politicians."[28]

In general, Americans are more willing to curtail civil liberties during times of crisis than during times of peace; civil libertarians argue that, given the wartime abuses of the past, it is during wartime that Americans should be most cautious about sacrificing their freedoms. Both sides, however, have plenty of hope that in the war on terrorism, the United States will learn from, rather than repeat, its past mistakes. As journalist Geoffrey Stone observes, "To strike the right balance in our time, our nation needs citizens who have the wisdom to know excess when they see it and the courage to stand for liberty when it is imperiled."[29]

Chapter Two

Patriotism and the First Amendment

In the war against terrorism, the United States is not about to pass another sedition act to make it illegal to criticize the government. But the war against terrorism could affect the First Amendment in other, less obvious ways. The First Amendment protects free expression, but it also protects the right of free assembly and freedom of the press. Civil libertarians are concerned that all three of these liberties could be abridged by homeland security measures.

Patriotism and Dissent

One of the main concerns of civil libertarians about the war against terrorism is the tension between patriotism and free speech. Historically, Americans have rallied around their government in times of war and crisis, and September 11 was no different. In the weeks after the terrorist attacks, the

United States experienced a surge in patriotism not seen since World War II, and President Bush's approval rating reached 90 percent.

Civil libertarians consider themselves patriots and do not object to Americans' expressing their love for their country. However, they caution that belligerent or overly aggressive patriotism—also known as jingoism—can lead to attacks on individuals who express a dissenting point of view. "Every war in American history, from the Revolution to the Gulf War, with the exception of World War II, inspired vigorous internal dissent,"[30] notes historian Eric Foner, and many such dissenters have historically been vilified, ostracized, and persecuted. Historian Bruce Watson notes that at the end of World War I, for example, "when a man refused to stand for the playing of the 'Star-Spangled Banner' at

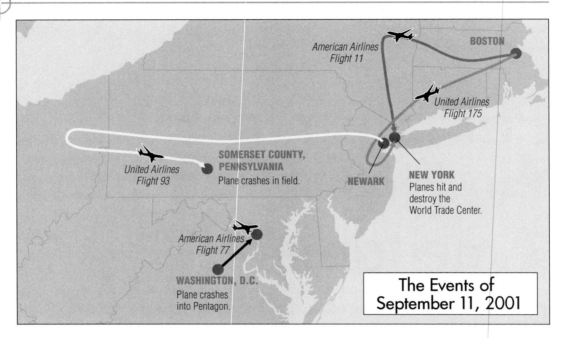

American Airlines
Flight 11

BOSTON

United Airlines
Flight 175

United Airlines
Flight 93

SOMERSET COUNTY,
PENNSYLVANIA
Plane crashes in field.

NEWARK

NEW YORK
Planes hit and
destroy the
World Trade Center.

American Airlines
Flight 77

WASHINGTON, D.C.
Plane crashes
into Pentagon.

The Events of
September 11, 2001

a May 6 [1919] pageant in Washington, D.C., a sailor shot him three times, and the audience burst into applause."[31]

Fortunately, nothing so violent happened to dissenters in the wake of September 11, but there were several examples of individuals being fired, harassed, or castigated for expressing their opinions. Dan Guthrie, a columnist for the *Daily Courier,* a local Oregon newspaper, and Tom Gutting, editor of the *Texas City Sun,* were both fired for writing columns suggesting that President Bush's failure to return to the White House immediately after the September 11 attacks was cowardly. And several ABC affiliates dropped comedian Bill Maher's *Politically Incorrect* talk show after a controversial comment he made comparing the U.S. bombing of Afghanistan to the September 11 attacks: "We have been the cowards lobbing cruise

missiles from 2,000 miles away. . . . Staying in the airplane when it hits the building, say what you want about it, that's not cowardly."[32] Several advertisers pulled their support for Maher's show, and it was later canceled.

Many peace activists protested Operation Enduring Freedom, the October 2001 invasion of Afghanistan, in which U.S. and British forces ousted the governing Taliban, which was believed to have aided al-Qaeda forces, from power. But the element of the war on terrorism that provoked the most dissent, and attacks on dissent, was the U.S. invasion of Iraq in spring 2003. Many celebrities were vilified for their antiwar views, and several country music stations boycotted the Dixie Chicks after they stated that they were ashamed of President Bush. At Wheaton College in Massachusetts, neighbors threw rocks through the windows of students who had hung the American flag upside down in protest against the invasion. After leading peace vigils in the town of Twenty-Nine Palms, California, Reverend Joseph Matoush found a note tacked to his church door that read "Why don't you leave America now."[33] And in March 2003, in a mall outside Albany, New York, lawyer Stephen E. Downs was arrested on trespassing charges after he refused to take off a T-shirt that said "Give peace a chance"— Downs had just purchased the T-shirt in the same mall he was arrested in.

A Chilling Climate for Free Speech

These incidents seem to have been relatively few and far between. And there have been no major incidents of the government censoring speech. Instead, such incidents have involved private citizens or groups rebuking other individuals for their opinions, which in many cases is not a violation of the First Amendment. For example, the advertisers who pulled their support for Bill Maher's talk show were exercising their

Many country music stations boycotted the music of the Dixie Chicks after the band denounced President Bush's decision to wage war on Iraq.

right to express disagreement with his controversial comments.

Nevertheless, civil libertarians worry that fear of being condemned for expressing one's views has created an atmosphere in which Americans are afraid to question or criticize the war on terrorism. "When we censor ourselves in the name of being good Americans we forsake the freedoms that make us unique," [34] writes Paul McMasters, ombudsman of the First Amendment Center. Historian Eric Foner echoes the idea that free speech can suffer even when the government has not explicitly suppressed dissent: "Self-imposed silence is as debilitating to democracy as censorship," [35] he writes.

Concerns over the right to dissent were exacerbated when President Bush proclaimed on September 20, 2001, "Either you are with us, or you are with the terrorists." [36] In the context of his speech, Bush was warning other nations not to aid or harbor terrorists. But the aggressive nature of the statement alarmed civil liberties groups. "The beginnings of a free-speech chill are evident," [37] warned *BusinessWeek*'s Ciro Scotti in a column written shortly after the speech.

The ACLU and other groups have also argued that the USA PATRIOT Act contributes to the "chilling" of free speech. The USA PATRIOT Act expands the definition of "terrorism" to include domestic activities (whereas previous definitions had covered only international terrorism). In some respects, the definitions of "domestic terrorism" are rather open-ended. Nancy Chang of the Center for Constitutional Rights points out the USA PATRIOT Act's definition of domestic terrorism includes acts that "appear to be intended . . . to influence the policy of a

---

The Dangers of Self-Censorship

In an October 2001 column, Mother Jones *writer Brooke Shelby Briggs expressed alarm at the reluctance of Americans to criticize government policies after September 11.*

"Far more surprising than government attempts to stifle criticism is the seeming willingness of the media, politicians, and activist groups—particularly those on the left—to censor *themselves*. Some may be backing off to avoid the kind of public crucifixion endured by *Politically Incorrect*'s Bill Maher. Others, however, apparently truly believe that frank and vibrant public discourse is damaging to the country's moral fiber. . . .

But if ever there's a time to critically examine the legitimacy and ability of a leader, it's when he is leading the nation into an open-ended war and asking citizens to 'make certain sacrifices,' including some of our freedoms. Like a muscle, free speech has to be exercised, or it weakens. . . .

Dissent . . . is more than a privilege and a right; it's a responsibility. By abdicating our responsibility to voice opposition, we invite the erosion of the very value system we claim to be protecting."

government by intimidation or coercion." Chang argues that "because this crime is couched in such vague and expansive terms, it may well be read by federal law enforcement agencies as licensing the investigation and surveillance of political activists and organizations based on their opposition to government policies. It also may be read by prosecutors as licensing the criminalization of legitimate political dissent."[38]

Other sections of the USA PATRIOT Act authorize the FBI and other agencies to conduct wiretaps and e-mail surveillance of groups that may be engaged in domestic terrorism, and civil libertarians suggest that this authorization could lead to government monitoring of environmental, antiabortion, and other groups that vigorously oppose government policies. Such monitoring could infringe not just on individual privacy, but also on the First Amendment's guarantee of freedom of assembly. Courts have interpreted the First Amendment to mean that the government may not discriminate against individuals based on the viewpoints they hold or the religious or political groups with which they associate. Therefore, argues the ACLU, it is unconstitutional for the government to investigate individuals for expressing their opinions or associating with political advocacy groups. The USA PATRIOT Act, an ACLU facts sheet states, "violates the First Amendment by effectively authorizing the FBI to investigate U.S. persons, including American citizens, based in part on their exercise of First Amendment activity."[39]

Government Secrecy and Freedom of the Press

Beyond individual freedom of speech, the war on terrorism also raises questions about the First Amendment's guarantee of freedom of the press, and whether that freedom may conflict with homeland security concerns. For journalists and civil libertarians, one of the most unsettling aspects of the war on terrorism is the atmosphere of secrecy that the government has adopted concerning security and counterterrorism measures.

On October 12, 2002, for example, Attorney General John Ashcroft issued a memorandum instructing federal agencies to refuse Freedom of Information Act (FOIA) requests unless clearly required to approve them by law. The FOIA is a law passed in 1966 that grants citizens the right to access any government document unless the document falls into one of nine specific categories of exemption. Prior to Ashcroft's memorandum, the general standard had been to grant FOIA requests to access documents unless doing so would cause "foreseeable harm." Essentially, the standard had been to grant FOIA requests unless there was a clear reason not to do so; now, after Ashcroft's memorandum, the standard is to *refuse* most FOIA requests. The Critical Infrastructure Information Act of 2002 further weakened FOIA by creating a new category of information—vulnerabilities in vital systems such as energy, transportation, and communication networks—that are exempt from FOIA requests.

Other examples of the government withholding information from the press include President Bush's decree on November 13, 2001, that suspected terrorists may be tried by secret military tribunals rather than civilian courts of law, and the government's refusal to release the names of prisoners captured in the fighting in Afghanistan and being held at U.S. military facilities in Guantánamo Bay, Cuba.

More generally, homeland security officials are hesitant to divulge any information about U.S. vulnerabilities for fear that terrorists might exploit them. Hundreds of thousands of documents—ranging from maps of a city's water mains to the blueprints of government buildings—have been pulled from government websites, and government officials often speak only in the vaguest terms when discussing security measures. Such information could potentially be of use to terrorists, and the First Amendment Center's McMasters agrees that "no reasonable person would argue that the press should be told every government secret." [40]

But some of the information being withheld, such as cities' emergency evacuation plans, is also valuable to the public. Civil libertarians worry that the government is overreacting in curtailing the public's access to government information.

In 2002 Attorney General John Ashcroft instructed federal agencies to restrict public access to government documents.

"We seem to be shifting to the public's need to know instead of the public's right to know," [41] says Gary Boss, director of a government watchdog group.

Open government and the free flow of information are two hallmarks of democracy. "The Constitution relies on an informed electorate to provide the ultimate check against arbitrary government,"[42] states the Lawyers Committee for Human Rights. Excessive government secrecy limits the ability of citizens to monitor, question, and criticize the actions of their elected leaders. Government secrecy also limits the ability of journalists to do their job of providing information to the public. In this sense, government secrecy conflicts with the First Amendment's guarantee of freedom of the press.

The Press's Role in Helping Americans Evaluate Government Policies

Defenders of open government and freedom of the press are not motivated solely by ideological concerns. From a purely pragmatic perspective, the secrecy surrounding homeland security measures makes it difficult—and in some cases, impossible—for the press to report on,

---

Patriotism and Conformity

Writing in the spring 2002 issue of Law and Contemporary Problems, *attorney Susan Gellman believes that since September 11 the greatest threat to free speech has not been government censorship, but rather the social pressure against criticizing the war on terrorism.*

"It truly cannot be said that government in the United States has responded to the current crisis by grossly restricting our First Amendment rights of speech, press, or religion. . . .

Government censorship and repression is not the only threat to the freedoms listed in the First Amendment. Think for a moment about what all those freedoms are about: protection of the one who disagrees with the majority, or who is different in some matter of ideology or belief. The Bill of Rights in general, the First Amendment in particular, acts as a safety valve on a majority-rules democracy. The tyranny of the majority can be every bit as oppressive as the tyranny of a monarch. . . .

When we feel a sense of threat and crisis, we feel an instinctive urge toward unity—closing the ranks, circling the wagons—lest divided we fall. This urge brings out some of the best in us: Witness the countless reports of heroism, neighborliness, and generosity following the September attacks.

. . .

But the impulse toward unity can bring out some scary things, too. Even in peacetime there is pressure to conform to positions and ideas seen by their adherents as pro-social and important, in the name of the greater good. . . . In time of crisis, though, the whole scale is ratcheted up several notches as the impulse toward unity becomes urgent. It no longer simply seems desirable that we all agree; it feels like unity is crucial to our safety and survival.

The tyranny of the majority makes itself felt through official action of a majoritarian government, but it also operates quite effectively through the more elusive forces of social pressure."

and for the public to evaluate, the government's security efforts. As Ken Paulson, senior vice president for the Freedom Forum, explains,

> There's no question that our society views public information in a dramatically different way after Sept. 11. There are legitimate concerns about whether public records may contain details that could abet a terrorist act. Yet if we're not comfortable with a public document which details an airport's security plan, how comfortable are we with no information at all and just an assertion by government officials to the effect of "Security plan? Sure, we've got one."?[43]

Excessive secrecy may diminish security if people are kept in the dark about what is being done to protect them. Obstacles to the flow of information have frequently been cited as contributing factors in the tragedy of September 11. For example, the FBI, CIA, and other agencies failed to share all their information about al-Qaeda with each other, and Congress and the public failed to demand more information about counterterrorism measures.

Some members of the news media caution that, when it comes to the war on terrorism, journalists themselves have not made enough of an effort to maintain objectivity and ask government officials the "tough questions" about U.S. policies. Many journalists naturally became caught up in the surge of patriotism that followed the September 11 attacks. Some television anchors began wearing red, white, and blue ribbons on their lapels and broadcasting with American flags in the background. Critics say that such shows of patriotism may give a progovernment bias to these programs' reporting. "We don't need our journalists to be waving flags," says columnist Norman Solomon, "we need our journalists not to speak for the U.S. government, but to speak to the crucial mission of journalists to . . . give us facts, give us information."[44]

Other journalists may fear that they will lose readers or viewers if they appear too critical of the government. But as longtime journalist Av Westin says, "I've always believed our job was to ask questions that need to be asked, regardless of official reaction or public opinion."[45] Bob Edwards, host of National Public Radio's *Morning Edition,* echoes the sentiment that journalists have a responsibility to inform the public: "Being popular might be good for business," he says, "but that is not our job. We are supposed to be surrogates for the public—the eyes and ears of citizens who don't have the access we have."[46]

Finally, many journalists are legitimately concerned that in reporting on security issues, they may inadvertently aid terrorists. This case was made forcefully by intelligence analyst Dennis Pluchinsky in a *Washington Post* article in which he charged the U.S. media with treason for reporting on U.S. vulnerabilities to terrorism and flaws in the government's security initiatives. "The president and Congress should pass laws temporarily restricting the media from

After the September 11 terrorist attacks, many Americans felt willing to surrender some First Amendment freedoms in the interest of national security.

publishing any security information that can be used by our enemies,"[47] he wrote. Free press advocates such as Ken Paulson of the Freedom Forum refute the need for such measures, arguing for journalistic restraint and responsibility rather than government censorship. "A free press can serve as an invaluable watchdog on government actions, without undercutting our national interests," he writes. "Reporters can ask tough questions while wearing flag lapel pins. Professionalism and patriotism can—and must—coexist."[48]

Shifting Attitudes on First Amendment Issues

The tension some journalists feel between supporting their government, on the one hand, and providing unbiased, aggressive reporting, on the other, is mirrored by the public's ambivalence toward many First Amendment issues. Each year, the First Amendment Center, in collaboration with *American Journalism Review*, conducts a "State of the First Amendment" survey, in which it polls a random sample of a thousand adults on various First Amendment issues. Its 2002 survey, the first taken after the September 11 attacks, uncovered some of the lowest levels of support for the First Amendment since the survey started in 1997. Nearly half of those surveyed said the First Amendment goes "too far" in the freedoms that it guarantees. Forty-two percent said that the press has too much freedom. More than 40 percent of those surveyed said that the press should not be allowed to freely criticize the military, and almost half said that the press had been too aggressive in asking government officials for information about the war on terrorism. Finally, 42 percent said that the government should be able to monitor Muslims, even if that means infringing on religious freedom.

These figures suggest that many Americans are willing to accept curtailment of their First Amendment rights if it furthers the war on terrorism. Yet 40 percent of respondents to the 2002 survey said that they had too little access to information about the war on terrorism, and 48 percent said that there was too little access to government records. "Apparently," note the authors of the 2002 report, "there is a 'disconnect' between public support for a free press and the actions [the public] expects the press to take in furtherance of this privilege."[49]

The findings of the First Amendment Center's 2003 survey showed some signs

The Press as a Watchdog of Government

In the summer 2003 issue of Neiman Reports, *journalist Paul McMasters argues that the press's role in questioning government policies and informing the public is more important than ever during wartime.*

"During times of national stress, when Congress is acquiescent, the courts deferential and the citizenry mute and afraid, the role of the press becomes even more vital. The press have a constitutional franchise not just because they report and deliver the news but because the ways in which they do this provide context, organize and prioritize information, and hold accountable those who are in power and

their policies. When the national agenda is set without active participation of the citizenry, informed by an independent press, the democratic process is compromised.

[For example,] as the Bush administration advanced its new policy of preemptive war and carried the nation along into the Iraq war, press coverage failed to fully explore the importance and scope of these developments. . . .

The press and its advocates must confront the hard reality that the press cannot serve as an instrument of freedom when they become a tool of government."

that, as the war on terrorism becomes a more routine part of American policy, support for civil liberties is on the rebound. Only one-third of respondents said that the First Amendment goes "too far" in the freedom it guarantees, although 42 percent still said that the press has too much freedom. Compared to the previous year, responses that the press had been too aggressive in asking government officials about the war on terrorism dropped 10 percent. However, one-third of respondents said that people should not be allowed to protest U.S. involvement in a war during a period of active military combat, and one-third also said that public school officials should be allowed to prohibit high school students from expressing their opinions about the war on school property.

Underlying all these issues is the question of whether Americans should limit the exercise of their First Amendment rights during times of national crisis. While Americans in general often express ambivalence about freedom of speech and freedom of the press, especially during wartime, civil libertarians wholeheartedly reject the idea that patriotism and the First Amendment are in conflict. For them, defending the most controversial wartime liberties—the freedom to dissent and the freedom of the press to further informed public discourse about the war effort—is in itself an exercise in patriotism.

Chapter Three

Government Surveillance and the Right to Privacy

The right to privacy is not mentioned explicitly anywhere in the Constitution. However, court rulings have suggested that a right to privacy is inherent in the Fourth Amendment's limits on government searches and the Fifth Amendment's protection against self-incrimination. Moreover, the Ninth Amendment specifically states that individuals have rights other than those enumerated in the Constitution. Supreme Court justice Louis Brandeis has written that the bedrock of the Bill of Rights is "the right to be let alone," [50] and many people feel this means that individuals have the right to remain anonymous unless authorities have reasonable cause to believe they have committed a crime.

One of the greatest civil liberties issues in the war on terrorism is the inherent tension between individuals' right to privacy and the government's need to identify and locate potential terrorists. Some of the most insidious crimes of terrorists, such as suicide bombings and airline hijackings, take advantage of their ability to become anonymous and blend in with a crowd. Even if the names and appearances of terrorists have been determined through intelligence and investigation operations, terrorists, like other criminals, may still evade detection through the use of disguises, forged credentials, or simply by "lying low" and not attracting attention to themselves. Therefore, the ability of law enforcement officials to establish an individual's identity is a key part of homeland security measures. Some of the means used to verify people's identities, however, have come under fire from privacy-rights groups.

ID Checkpoints and Watch Lists

One of the first steps taken after September 11 was to enact stricter procedures for identification (ID) checks at airports and border crossings. Such checkpoints, however, are not a security panacea. First, ID credentials can be faked. Second, ID checkpoints are useless if terrorists can circumvent them and gain access to a building or events through some unnoticed hole in security. Finally, it is impractical to set up effective ID checkpoints at every conceivable terrorist target.

To supplement ID checkpoints, security officials usually keep "watch lists" with

Checkpoints, like this one at Los Angeles International Airport, add some measure of security for travelers, but they are not foolproof.

the photos of suspected criminals, including terrorists. Of course, watch lists are prone to human error. On the one hand, in a crowd, it is easy for security officials to miss the individuals on the watch lists. On the other hand, security officials may also mistakenly detain, search, or even arrest anyone who looks like the suspects on their watch lists. Civil libertarians worry that security officials may engage in ethnic profiling, harassing Arab and Arab-looking individuals based solely on their appearance.

Picking Terrorists Out of a Crowd

One proposed solution to both the vulnerabilities of ID checkpoints and the shortcomings of watch lists is facial-recognition technology (FRT). FRT combines video surveillance cameras with special software in order to automatically scan crowds for wanted individuals. The video cameras capture images of people's faces, which are automatically compared against a database of wanted individuals, and the FRT system alerts authorities if a match is found. After September 11, FRT was implemented at airports in Boston, Rhode Island, California, and Florida. It was also used at the 2001 Super Bowl in Tampa, Florida.

Advocates of FRT say that it automates and improves on the current system of watch lists. They point out that the technology cannot identify just anyone, but rather only those individuals listed in the database to which the FRT system is linked. In September 2001, the then-president of Visionics Corporation, Joseph Atick, stated that the FaceIt surveillance system, his own company's version of the technology, "does not identify you or me. It is simply an alarm that alerts when a terrorist on a watch list passes through [an entrance] at an airport."[51]

Advocates of such systems also argue that they benefit civil liberties by reducing the likelihood of discrimination and ethnic profiling by security agents. "Face recognition machines," writes Harvard law professor Alan Dershowitz, "are certainly preferable to ethnic stereotyping, which is simply a primitive, human method of face identification."[52]

"Big Brother Is Watching You"

Despite its potential to reduce ethnic profiling, many civil liberties groups maintain that FRT and other video surveillance of the public is an invasion of privacy. The American Civil Liberties Union (ACLU) states that people "have the right to know if their movements and identities are being captured"[53] and warns that if public video surveillance becomes widespread it "will have a chilling effect on public life."[54]

Privacy advocate Sonia Arrison expands on this idea. She worries that video surveillance of public spaces will encourage conformity and stifle individual expression because people who know they are being watched or who fear the government will

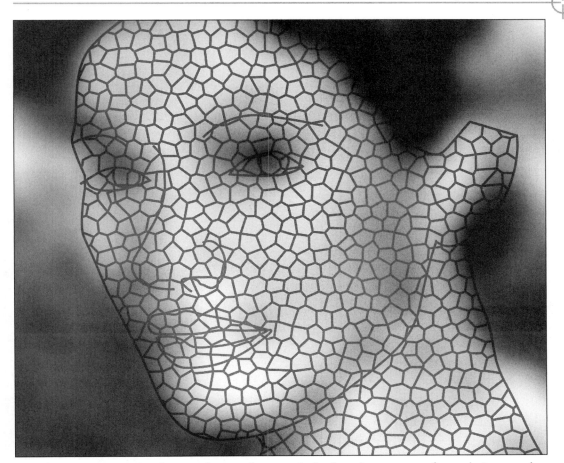

Facial-recognition technology is designed to match the facial structures of people in crowds with images of wanted individuals stored in a database.

misuse the information will act differently. She writes that such surveillance

> can be used to pressure individuals into acting according to majority norms because they worry they will be identified and persecuted. For example, a Muslim may not walk into a mosque, or a gay couple may avoid public displays of affection. . . . Systematic surveillance of Americans by government is something to avoid if we wish to maintain the freedoms that define this country.[55]

For many critics of FRT, the prospect of widespread video surveillance is too reminiscent of Big Brother in George Orwell's novel *1984*. *1984* depicts a dark future in which a totalitarian government monitors the movements, actions, and even the thoughts of its citizens. Big Brother is the symbol of the government that rules the world of *1984*, a government

Biometric Identifiers

Facial-recognition technology (FRT) is a biometric system. A biometric system uses a personal trait, physical characteristic, or combination thereof to identify an individual. In the case of FRT systems, the biometric identifier is the face. Individuals may alter their appearance, but many aspects of a person's face—such as the distance between the eyes, the width of the mouth, and hundreds of other measurements—are largely immutable. Taken together, these facial measurements form a unique "faceprint," and in fact traditional police fingerprinting is another example of a biometric system. More sophisticated biometric systems may use retinal scans or voice-recognition technology, while the photographs used in driver's licenses or police mug shots are basic forms of biometric identification.

The advantage of FRT over other forms of biometric systems is that FRT can be employed from a distance. Individuals must wait in line at security checkpoints to show photo IDs or have their thumbprint scanned, and security officials must guard against anyone getting around the security checkpoints. In contrast, FRT cameras can be placed throughout a building. In theory, FRT cameras could be used both to guard every entrance to an area and to scan the crowds of people who have already gained access to the secure area.

that knows everything about the people under its rule. In the world of *1984,* huge posters proclaiming "Big Brother Is Watching You" are everywhere, as are "telescreens" that record everything that people do. Authors David Kopel and Michael Krause argue that, like the telescreens in *1984,* "widespread face scanning could eventually make it possible for the government to track the movement of most citizens most of the time." [56]

Though currently in use as an experimental technology, FRT faces many technical hurdles before it becomes either the security solution its advocates envision or the threat to privacy its critics fear. "So far, computer-recognition systems have achieved only 5 to 10 percent of the accuracy of the human eye," [57] writes *Science World* reporter Libby Tucker. In tests of FRT, the systems often fail to identify the target individuals, while incorrectly zeroing in on others. FRT systems, like human security guards, can also be fooled when the target individual wears sunglasses, sports facial hair, or otherwise covers his or her face. The technology for facial recognition systems is constantly improving, but at airports and other areas where security is a concern, driver's licenses and other credentials are still the primary means of verifying a person's identity.

The Debate over a National ID Card

September 11 exposed many of the flaws of the United States's systems for issuing driver's licenses and other IDs. As Marti

Dinerstein, president of the public policy firm Immigration Matters, notes, "The issue of secure identification became a national concern in the United States after it was discovered that all 19 September 11 hijackers had valid or fake Social Security numbers and 18 of the 19 had authentic or phony driver's licenses or motor vehicle ID cards."[58] Seven of the terrorists, for example, were able to obtain nondriver's ID cards from the Virginia Department of Motor Vehicles (DMV), which at the time did not require applicants to provide proof of residency. The state has since closed that particular loophole, but the Virginia example is only part of a much broader problem. An October 2002 *Government Computer News* article notes that "there are about 240 different driver's licenses formats in use across the 50 states today"[59] and that it is almost

A woman obtains a driver's license. Most of the terrorists involved in the September 11 attacks obtained identification cards with fraudulent information.

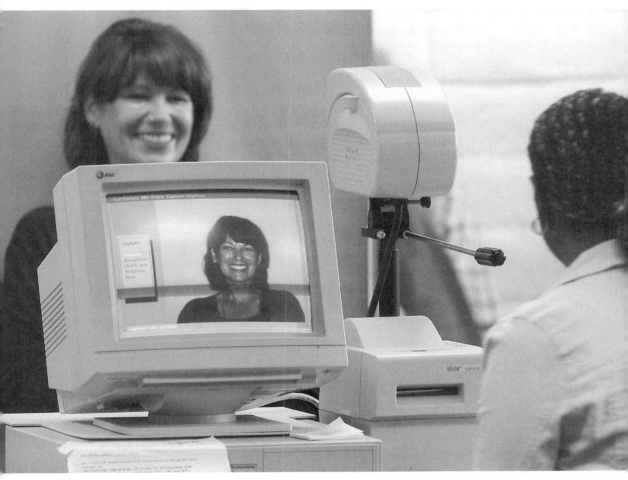

impossible for a security official to be truly knowledgeable about each one of them.

Given the easy availability of phony driver's licenses and other forms of ID in various states, many policy analysts have suggested that a national ID card should replace the current driver's license system. It does not make sense, they argue, that driver's licenses—issued by local DMVs that deal primarily with tasks such as driver testing and vehicle registration—are the most accepted proof of identification in the United States. "You can't get on a plane today without a driver's license or passport. A national ID card would perform the same function but with a great deal more accuracy and security," [60] writes James Glassman of the American Enterprise Institute.

Americans, however, have historically opposed the idea of a national ID card. In 1996, when uniform national driver's license standards were enacted into law, Congress responded to public criticism and quickly repealed the standards. Referring to the appeal, Representative Dick Armey proclaimed, "This is a classic victory of freedom over 'Big Brother.' Because we acted quickly, no American will have to carry a national ID card. A national driver's license . . . is more suited to a police state than to a free country." [61] Some civil libertarians fear that a national ID system would require individuals to provide proof of identification whenever they travel, apply for a job, or make a major purchase. This will make it easier, they argue, for the federal government to track where citizens go and what they do. "National IDs threaten liberty and anonymity," [62] writes Clyde Wayne Crews Jr. of the libertarian Cato Institute.

Supporters of national ID cards reject such fears. "We must identify ourselves for any number of activities in daily life," argues *U.S. News & World Report*'s Randall Stross, "so the only freedom that would be lost with the advent of improved ID technology is the freedom to falsify one's legal identity." [63]

As to the question of the right to anonymity, Harvard professor Dershowitz

Some Americans believe that national identification cards, like those used in Hong Kong, should also be used in the United States.

maintains that "I don't believe we can afford to recognize such a right in this age of terrorism. No such right is hinted at in the Constitution. And though the Supreme Court has identified a right to privacy, privacy and anonymity are not the same."[64]

Improving State-Issued Driver's Licenses

The movement for a national ID card seemed strong in the weeks after September 11. But as *Newsweek* reports, by May 2002 it had lost momentum: "An alliance of right and left [argued] that a national ID card was anathema [*strongly* opposed] to traditional privacy values. The Bush administration said it had no interest in such a system. Civil liberties groups kept hitting the Big Brother issue and the public seemed to agree."[65] But although the movement for a national ID card has stalled, efforts to develop a better nationwide identification system have not.

Since September 11, more than twenty states have enacted legislation to improve driver's license security. States such as Virginia have made the application process for obtaining state ID cards more rigorous, and many states have made the cards they issue harder to counterfeit, using holograms, watermarks, and high-definition photographs. Some states are also using biometric identifiers to ensure driver identity. California, Colorado, Florida, Georgia, Hawaii, Texas, and West Virginia all collect fingerprints from driver's license applicants. West Virginia also uses FRT to verify a dri-

ver's identity during renewal, and other states are planning to follow its lead.

Few object to these DMV reforms. More controversial, however, is the movement to transform driver's licenses into "smart cards" that can store information about an individual in a computer chip embedded in the card. The American Association of Motor Vehicle Administrators (AAMVA) is pushing state governments to adopt uniform standards for storing information on driver's licenses. If different states would adopt these standards, then universal card readers could be installed at security checkpoints in airports and government buildings to allow security officials to verify the authenticity of the cards.

Connecting Watch Lists

The AAMVA is also encouraging state DMVs to link their driver's license databases. This is part of a larger effort by homeland security officials to make it easier for different government agencies and different levels of government to share information quickly and easily. The potential of interconnected databases, in conjunction with smart ID cards, to prevent terrorism is best illustrated by example. On August 23, 2001, two of the September 11 hijackers, Khallad al-Mihdhar and Nawaf al-Hazmi, were put on the CIA watch list of persons to be denied entry into the country. However, by that time both men had already entered the United States and obtained state-issued photo IDs in multiple states. Beginning on August 27, 2001,

Will State Driver's Licenses Become National IDs?

The Electronic Privacy Information Center (EPIC) opposes a national ID card system on the grounds that it will erode individual privacy. In its February 2002 position paper "Your Papers, Please: From the State Drivers License to a National Identification System," EPIC argues that the movement to standardize state driver's licenses holds many of the same threats to privacy as a national ID card.

"The American Association of Motor Vehicle Administrators (AAMVA) Special Task Force on Identification Security has issued recommendations that would turn the state driver license into a de facto national ID card. The proposed scheme . . . would facilitate greater information sharing between jurisdictions and with state and federal agencies. It seeks to reduce fraud by encoding unique biometric identifiers on licenses and strictly enforcing prohibitions on credential fraud. But the biometric identifier would also enable new systems of identification in the private sector, and will contribute to greater profiling and surveillance of American citizens.

EPIC supports efforts to detect and prevent fraud occurring by means of the state driver's license. New technologies can reduce the risk of counterfeiting and fraud. It is also appropriate for the state Departments of Motor Vehicles (DMVs) to implement improved document security measures to prevent forgery. However, EPIC opposes AAMVA's move to standardize driver's licenses, to collect more and more invasive personal information, and to expand the information sharing capacities of DMVs. This proposal has all the elements, risks and dangers of a national identification card system. The only distinctions between the AAMVA proposal and other National ID proposals rejected in the past are that (a) the card will not be issued by the federal government but by state motor vehicle agencies under mandatory federal regulations, and (b) the driver's license and DMV issued identity cards, held by 228 million individuals, are not (yet) mandatory. These distinctions are illusory rather than substantive, do not diminish the harm to individuals' privacy, and should not dissuade public opposition to the scheme."

---

the FBI began an investigation to locate the two men. Nevertheless, both men were able to use their state-issued IDs to board the flight that crashed into the Pentagon.

At the time, the CIA did not have procedures in place for quickly sharing its watch list with the FBI, let alone all of the nation's airport security personnel. Of course, many reforms have been implemented since then. But with the system of smart ID cards and interconnected databases that homeland security planners envision, the names of al-Mihdhar and al-Hazmi could have been disseminated to card readers almost instantly—essentially connecting the CIA's watch list with that of the airport's security personnel—and the two would-be hijackers would have raised security alarms upon attempting to enter the airport.

While it has enormous potential to enhance security, the system of smart cards and interconnected government databases alarm civil libertarians. State-issued smart ID cards, after all, are very much like the national ID cards that so many privacy advocates oppose. Critics argue that individuals would inevitably be required to show their smart ID cards, just like a national ID card, not just at airports, but wherever security is a concern. And as privacy advocate Mar Rotenburg explains, "Every time you swipe [a smart card], it leaves a record."[66]

By compiling all those records, law enforcement authorities could track the movements of any citizen. Even worse, according to privacy advocates, law enforcement databases could then potentially be linked to databases that contain individuals' financial, employment, and medical records. The United States would come a step closer to enabling the government to know almost everything about its citizens, just like Orwell's Big Brother in *1984*. "To some, the scariest privacy prospect is a big centralized national database (or a series of linked ones) that has all the goods on almost everybody,"[67] writes *Newsweek*'s Steven Levy.

Total Information Awareness

This "big centralized database" is essentially what the U.S. Department of Defense is trying to create with its Terrorism Information Awareness (TIA) project. TIA aims to create software that will use a technique known as data mining to allow law enforcement agents to quickly search information that is stored in countless government databases throughout the country. TIA will not actually collect the information into one database, but the effect will be much the same.

When TIA initially became public in late 2002, it was called the Total Information

The two hijackers who crashed the plane into the Pentagon had state-issued identification that was checked as they boarded the flight.

Awareness project, and its Orwellian name instantly raised the ire of civil libertarians. "TIA may be the closest thing to a true 'Big Brother' program that has ever been contemplated in the United States,"[68] warned the ACLU. Even the rather conservative columnist William Safire called TIA a "supersnoop's dream" and warned that it would give the government the ability to monitor "every purchase you make with a credit card, every magazine subscription you buy and medical prescription you fill, every Web site you visit and e-mail you send or receive, every academic grade you receive, every bank deposit you make, every trip you book and every event you attend."[69]

Some critics charge that TIA amounts to a violation of the Fourth Amendment, which protects individuals against unreasonable searches. James Harper, editor of the privacy website privacilla.org, charges that "the idea behind TIA is something akin to a permanent, institutional search of our papers and effects."[70]

Homeland security officials were taken aback by the intensity of the backlash against TIA. The project's defenders vehemently denied that TIA will be used to spy on Americans. They point out that TIA will not give the government access to any information it does not already have, but instead will only allow federal agents to access that information more quickly, an improvement that would be a great boon to homeland security efforts. "The goal is to enable investigators to amass in minutes clues that now could take weeks or months to collect,"[71] writes *National Journal* writer Stuart Taylor Jr.

As to the civil libertarians' concerns about the Fourth Amendment, TIA defenders cite Supreme Court precedents that have ruled that individuals cannot expect information that they voluntarily give to others—such as when they use a credit card instead of cash for purchases or enter their phone number or e-mail address on a website form—to remain private. And, they maintain, TIA will merely enable the government to access this information more easily. As lawyer Solveig Singleton explains,

George Orwell's *1984* warns of the dangers of a government with too much control over the lives of its citizens.

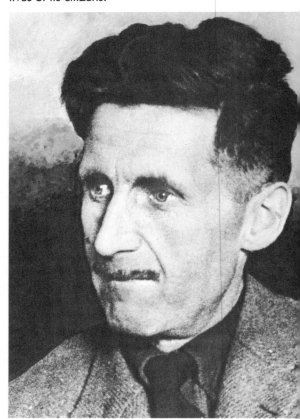

The Danger of Domestic Spying

As New Republic writer Jeffrey Rosen explains, one reason people oppose a government that knows everything about its people is the fear that such a government would have the evidence to prosecute many citizens for minor violations of the law.

"There is nothing inherently objectionable about increasing the power of federal officials to engage in domestic surveillance, as long as those powers are limited to the investigation and prosecution of terrorists. Domestic surveillance becomes dangerous, however, when federal officials are allowed to spy on millions of citizens suspected not of terrorism but of low-level crimes, such as drug offenses or illegally downloading copyrighted music. If the government insists on unrestricted access to our credit-card histories, Internet browsing, international phone calls, and bookstore purchases, who among us couldn't be prosecuted or embarrassed by some low-level wrongdoing? . . .

The [best] way to balance privacy and security in a world of integrated databases is to limit the use of evidence discovered in general data searches to the prosecution of terrorism and to prohibit the government from using it to prosecute low-level crimes."

"The Fourth Amendment does not say that the government may not collect, keep or store information."[72]

Power and Its Abuse

Information is power. FRT, smart ID cards, and the TIA project all give the government more power in the form of information. This power may be vital in preventing future terrorist acts. But it may also be abused—for example, if the government were to use surveillance and tracking mechanisms to monitor and investigate dissenting individuals or political, religious, or ethnic groups. As security and law enforcement officials adopt new surveillance and computer technologies, civil libertarians hope that the government also adopts and enforces rules and oversight mechanisms to prevent their abuse.

Chapter Four

The PATRIOT Act and the Fourth Amendment

The law enforcement officials charged with preventing another terrorist attack on America face a daunting challenge. Terrorists have the element of surprise: It is likely that there will be little or no prior warning of when, where, or how the next attack will occur. Guarding U.S. targets against terrorist attacks is, therefore, very difficult. Rather than trying to protect every possible target, one of America's primary strategies in preventing terrorism is to identify terrorists and learn of their plans before they are carried out.

To do this, law enforcement and intelligence agencies such as the FBI and CIA use a variety of surveillance and search techniques. In addition to having law enforcement agents follow and monitor suspected terrorists and perform physical searches of their homes or headquarters, these agencies may tap phones, monitor Internet use and e-mail, use electronic eavesdropping devices, and inspect suspects' financial, credit card, student, employment, and other records.

Law enforcement's authority to employ these search and surveillance techniques is restricted by the U.S. Constitution's Fourth Amendment, which states that

> the right of the people to be secure in their persons, houses, papers, and effects, against unreasonable searches and seizures, shall not be violated, and no warrants shall issue, but upon probable cause, supported by oath or affirmation, and particularly describing the place to be searched, and the persons or things to be seized.

Modern courts interpret this to mean that law enforcement agencies must normally obtain warrants to conduct searches. To obtain warrants, law enforcement agents must usually demonstrate "probable cause" to a judge—that is, show that they have reasonable grounds for suspecting an individual of committing a crime. As the Center for Constitutional Rights (CCR) explains, "The Fourth Amendment ensures that law enforcement agencies and officers do not act maliciously or conduct investigations where no credible evidence of wrongdoing exists."[73]

The Wall Between Intelligence Gathering and Law Enforcement

These Fourth Amendment protections apply to almost all criminal investigations conducted by law enforcement agencies, from local police departments to the FBI. However, intelligence investigations aimed at deterring espionage and other activities—including terrorism—are different. As the *Wall Street Journal*'s Brendan Miniter explains,

> Intelligence investigations . . . don't have these civil liberty protections. Investigators need only show evidence that a person may be involved in gathering information for a "foreign power," which includes al Qaeda. And search warrants are much broader for intelligence investigations, which allow agents to search homes or businesses or use wire taps, read e-mail and regular mail for months. And there is no natural check on this power, even the

target of an investigation is often blissfully unaware of snooping federal agents.[74]

The key difference is that spying has historically been justified as a tool of national security rather than law enforcement, to be used against "foreign powers" rather than ordinary citizens.

In the 1960s and 1970s, a series of journalistic and congressional investigations revealed that since the 1950s the government had abused its intelligence operations, using the CIA, FBI, and other agencies to spy on organizations and individuals—such as Martin Luther King Jr. and Vietnam War protesters—that, though controversial, were clearly not agents of foreign governments. In 1978, in an attempt to curb Fourth Amendment violations that had occurred in the name of counterespionage, Congress passed the Foreign Intelligence Surveillance Act (FISA).

FISA, along with several other reforms of the 1960s and 1970s, established a "wall" between intelligence gathering and law enforcement. The CIA was prohibited from engaging in domestic counterintelligence operations, and a legal framework was developed to govern how the FBI would conduct them instead. FISA banned warrantless searches of individuals suspected of being agents of foreign powers (according to the law, a "group engaged in international terrorism" is considered a "foreign power"). Instead, searches have to be approved by the Foreign Intelligence Surveillance Court (FISC), a secret court established by FISA.

To protect against Fourth Amendment violations, law enforcement agencies, such as this unit using facial-recognition technology, do not participate in intelligence gathering.

As long as the primary purpose of a search is to gather intelligence on foreign powers and their agents, then FISC allows the FBI to ignore many Fourth Amendment restrictions, such as having to show probable cause. But the FBI is largely prohibited from using evidence gathered in intelligence cases to prosecute criminal cases, and when intelligence and criminal investigations overlap, they come under severe scrutiny from FISC.

Investigations of suspected terrorists often fit this category.

Tearing Down the Wall

Many civil libertarians say that the wall between intelligence gathering and law enforcement is necessary to prevent the government from spying on Americans, as it did in the 1960s and 1970s. But many government officials argue that the wall has hindered counterterrorism efforts and was a major factor in the FBI's failure to prevent the September 11 attacks. The most notable case is that of Zacaria Moussaoui, an al-Qaeda agent who aided the September 11 hijackers while they were

The Origins of the Foreign Intelligence Surveillance Act

In the following excerpt from its September 2003 report "Assessing the New Normal: Liberty and Security for the Post–September 11 United States," the Lawyers Committee for Human Rights explains the circumstances behind the enactment of the Foreign Intelligence Surveillance Act (FISA), which regulates the government's authority to conduct domestic intelligence operations.

"FISA was one of the reform measures adopted in response to a 1976 report by the U.S. Senate Select Committee to Study Governmental Operations with Respect to Intelligence Activities (the Church Committee). The report revealed that on the premise of 'national security,' U.S. intelligence agencies had been carrying out illegal surveillance of domestic organizations, collecting 'vast amounts of information about the intimate details of citizens' lives and about their participation in legal and peaceful political activities.' Although the targets of this surveillance were primarily antiwar protesters and civil rights activists (including Dr. Martin Luther King, Jr.), they spanned a broad spectrum of groups, including the Women's Liberation Movement, the John Birch Society, and the American Christian Action Council.

The Church Committee determined that such abuses were an inevitable outgrowth of the executive branch's 'excessive' power over intelligence activities, which, until then, had been largely exempted from the normal system of checks and balances. This problem had its roots in the mid 1930s [and] ... grew substantially during the Cold War and during the civil unrest of the 1960s and 1970s. In the latter period, secret surveillance techniques that had been used against suspected Communist agents began to be applied against a wide range of domestic groups advocating for peaceful societal change, groups with no suspected connection to a foreign power. The Church Committee warned that the 'system for controlling intelligence must be brought back within the constitutional scheme,' emphasizing that 'unless new and tighter controls are established by legislation, domestic intelligence activities threaten to undermine our democratic society and fundamentally alter its nature.'"

in the United States. Prior to September 11, some government agents were suspicious of Moussaoui because he had attended a flight school where he inquired whether cockpit doors could be opened during flight and because he had spent time in Pakistan, where al-Qaeda recruits many operatives. But because the FBI could not demonstrate probable cause, it could not obtain a warrant to search Moussaoui's computer or tap his phone. "Consequently," writes Mark Reibling, author of a book on FBI-CIA relations, "the FBI lost its best chance to learn of Moussaoui's links to the other September 11 conspirators before they could strike."[75]

Inquiries into the government's counterterrorism efforts before September 11 have revealed other instances in which the CIA, FBI, and other agencies failed to share critical information with one another, in part because of the many rules against doing so. Weeks after the attacks, Attorney General John Ashcroft asserted that "tearing down the wall between intelligence and criminal information is one of the most important steps we will make or we will be able to take."[76]

Many parts of the USA PATRIOT Act are aimed at reducing the wall by expanding the FBI's FISA powers. For example, section 218 of the USA PATRIOT Act authorizes FBI agents to obtain search warrants without probable cause in investigations where intelligence gathering is a significant purpose of the investigation rather than the primary purpose, as originally stated in FISA. According to Robert

Levy of the libertarian Cato Institute, "This is not a trivial change. It means easier government access to personal and business records, and relaxed authorization of surveillance and wiretaps."[77]

Section 218 is just one of many parts of the USA PATRIOT Act that homeland security officials and civil libertarians are divided over. Ashcroft says that section 218 "makes the utilization of wiretaps against terrorists much more workable and will facilitate greater coordination between law enforcement and the intelligence side of our investigative resources."[78] But civil libertarians argue that section 218 undercuts one of the original purposes of FISA, which was to prevent FBI officials from too easi-

Fourth Amendment restrictions kept the FBI from monitoring Zacaria Moussaoui, an al-Qaeda agent who aided the September 11 hijackers.

ly sidestepping the Fourth Amendment's probable cause requirement.

The wall is further lowered by section 203 of the USA PATRIOT Act, which makes it easier for the FBI, CIA, and other agencies to share information obtained in both criminal and intelligence investigations. Again, FISA had specifically made it illegal for evidence gathered through intelligence operations—evidence gathered without adherence to Fourth Amendment restrictions—to be used in criminal cases. Nancy Chang of the Center for Constitutional Rights objects most to the fact that this sharing of information is not subject to judicial oversight: "While some additional sharing of information between agencies is undoubtedly appropriate given the nature of the terrorist threats we face," she writes, "the Act fails to protect us from the dangers posed to our political freedoms and our privacy when sensitive personal information is widely shared without court supervision." [79]

Secret Searches, Lack of Oversight

Section 213 of the USA PATRIOT Act empowers federal agents to conduct "sneak-and-peek" searches—covert searches of a person's home or office that are conducted without notifying the person until well after the search has been completed. FISA had authorized sneak-and-peek warrants in certain types of intelligence investigations, but the USA PATRIOT Act allows such warrants to be issued in any criminal investigation, even those that have noth-

ing to do with terrorism. Critics argue that this provision is far too broad. According to *Slate.com* editors Dahlia Lithwick and Julia Turner,

> The parts of the PATRIOT Act that rankle most are those provisions that sweep normal criminal law enforcement under the looser procedural standards for fighting terror. It's important that the state be able to fight terror. No one disputes this. But it's equally important that the state not use the war on terror to gut the warrant requirement. [80]

Bills have been introduced in Congress that would amend section 213 to implement more specific standards for when sneak-and-peek searches are justified.

Another type of secret search is authorized by section 215 of the USA PATRIOT Act, which grants federal agents the power to require third parties to turn over individuals' personal information without their knowledge or consent. For example, under section 215 the FBI could request a person's financial records from a bank, medical records from a doctor, or even a list of books that the person has checked out from a library. In addition, it would be illegal for the bank, doctor, or library to tell the individual in question about the search. (Some libraries have stopped keeping permanent records in order to protest this part of the act.) As with sneak-and-peek searches, FISA had already granted this power to FBI agents in special circumstances, but section 215 allows agents to access personal records

Judicial Oversight of Law Enforcement Authorities

Civil libertarians argue that one of the most alarming aspects of the USA PATRIOT Act is that it shifts the system of checks and balances on which the U.S. government is built. As noted in the ACLU's report Insatiable Appetite: The Government's Demand for New and Unnecessary Powers After September 11, *several parts of the USA PATRIOT Act empower the executive branch of government and weaken the judicial branch by removing judicial oversight from the law enforcement procedures.*

"Both the USA PATRIOT Act and the subsequent executive actions undermine the role of the judiciary in overseeing the exercise of executive authority. The Act essentially codifies a series of short cuts for government agents. Under many of its provisions, a judge exercises no review function whatsoever; the court must issue an order granting access to sensitive information upon mere certification by a government official. The Act reflects a distrust of the judiciary as an independent safeguard against abuse of executive authority. This trend is particularly apparent in the electronic surveillance provisions of the Act. For example, the USA PATRIOT Act subjects surveillance of Internet communications to a minimal standard of review. This surveillance would reveal the persons with whom one corresponded by e-mail and the websites one visited. Law enforcement agents may access this information by merely certifying that the information is relevant to an ongoing investigation. The court must accept the law enforcement certification; the judge must issue the order even if he or she finds the certification factually unpersuasive. . . .

These initiatives misunderstand the role of the judiciary in our constitutional system. They treat the courts as an inconvenient obstacle to executive action rather than an essential instrument of accountability."

as long as a senior-level Department of Justice official certifies that such an action will protect against international terrorism.

Under section 215, applications to gain access to personal records must be made to an FISC judge, but under the terms of the USA PATRIOT Act the judge has little authority to deny the FBI request. To civil libertarians, this is by far the most objectionable part of section 215. The purpose of search warrants is to include the courts in law enforcement, so that judges can ensure that police and FBI agents do not abuse their search powers.

Yet another provision of the USA PATRIOT Act, section 505, empowers the attorney general to order an individual to turn over personal records, including telephone logs, e-mails, and financial records. Before the USA PATRIOT Act, the attorney general had to have reasonable suspicion that the target individual was engaged in espionage to subpoena records in this manner, but under the USA PATRIOT Act the attorney general can use this power on anyone, without judicial oversight. Lithwick and Turner write that this power "is actually a good deal scarier than [section] 2153 . . . because there is no check on the attorney general's discretion."[81]

Justification for the New Powers

Critics of the USA PATRIOT Act point out that it was passed less than seven weeks after the September 11 attacks. In congressional terms, this is relatively fast, and critics say that some of the more worrisome parts of the act are due to the haste with which it was debated. Partially easing their concerns is the fact that many parts of the USA PATRIOT Act

are temporary measures: Sections 215, 218, and 505 are set to expire in October 2005. However, section 213, which authorizes sneak-and-peek searches, and part of section 203, which eases restrictions on the sharing of intelligence information among federal agencies, are permanent.

Attorney General Ashcroft and President Bush have indicated that they want to extend the powers set to expire, and add new ones, by passing the Domestic Security Enhancement Act, often referred to as "PATRIOT II." Speaking before the FBI Academy in September 2003, Bush said that "the PATRIOT Act imposed tough new penalties on terrorists and those who support them. But as the fight against terrorists progressed, we have found areas where more help is required."[82]

In August 2003, Attorney General Ashcroft embarked on a nationwide speaking

Police arrest a woman protesting the USA PATRIOT Act. Despite criticism of some of its provisions, many Americans support the act.

tour to explain how the USA PATRIOT Act has benefited law enforcement. "The Patriot Act gave agencies like the FBI and the CIA the ability to integrate their capabilities," he said in one speech. "It gave government the ability to 'connect the dots,' revealing the shadowy terrorist network in our midst." [83] The Bush administration also set up a website, www.lifeandliberty.gov, that seeks to dispel some of the concerns about the act.

There are many parts of the USA PATRIOT Act that empower law enforcement without raising serious civil liberties concerns. Section 219, for example, allows federal judges to issue nationwide search warrants in terrorism investigations, whereas previously federal agents had to expend precious time petitioning multiple judges in multiple districts for warrants. Other important provisions of the act clarify how 1970s-era regulations about wiretaps apply to the Internet.

Many Americans, in fact, support the USA PATRIOT Act. David Yepsen of the *Des Moines Register* maintains that "most Americans support the act because they understand that a nation must take special measures to survive in wartime. Had the act been in place prior to Sept. 11, the tragic events of that day might have been prevented." [84] And Richard Lowry of the *New York Post* charges that civil libertarians who attack the USA PATRIOT Act have "forgotten the importance of aggressive, preemptive law enforcement." [85]

An Ongoing Debate

But taken together, the USA PATRIOT Act's easing of Fourth Amendment search warrant restrictions, the sharing of intelligence information between the FBI and the CIA, and the lack of judicial oversight alarm privacy advocates and government watchdog groups. "To an unprecedented degree," writes Chang, "the Act sacrifices our political freedoms in the name of national security and upsets the democratic values that define our nation by consolidating vast new powers in the executive branch of government." [86]

Search and surveillance powers are the most powerful weapons the government has in the war on terrorism; they are also potentially grave threats to individual privacy and the rights enshrined in the Fourth Amendment. With some provisions of the USA PATRIOT Act set to expire in 2005 and with "PATRIOT II" on the horizon, clearly the debate over federal agents' expanded powers is far from over. Echoing the feeling of many Americans who feel ambivalent about the expanded search powers, former assistant attorney general Viet Dinh has commended the ongoing debate over the USA PATRIOT Act. Likening the war on terrorism to a footrace, Dinh says that the USA PATRIOT Act was passed in the "sprint phase" of the race, but now the United States must settle in for the "marathon phase" and determine what policies are best for the long haul. "Somewhere in this marketplace of ideas, of truths and half-truths, of fact and spin, we get a . . . picture of what the [Justice] Department should be doing," says Dinh. "The debate is healthy to establish the rules of this continuing path toward safety." [87]

Chapter Five

Discrimination Against Minorities and Immigrants

"The Hun within our gates is the worst of the foes of our own household," warned former president Theodore Roosevelt as America fought Germany during World War I. "Hun" was a slur used to refer to Germans, and Roosevelt was concerned that both newly arrived German immigrants and Americans of German descent might seek to undermine the U.S. war effort. "Every disloyal native-born American should be disfranchised and interned," said Roosevelt. "It is time to strike our enemies at home heavily and quickly." [88] Roosevelt's comments reflected the anti-German sentiment and general xenophobia, or fear of foreigners, that was prevalent in the United States at the time. Such senti-

ments led to widespread discrimination and ethnic bashing against German, Italians, and other minorities throughout World War I. The United States experienced a similar wave of xenophobia again during World War II, when the Japanese bombing of Pearl Harbor led the U.S. government to intern more than 110,000 Americans of Japanese ancestry, many of the them U.S. citizens.

Anti-Muslim Violence and Discrimination

Throughout U.S. history, during war and other times of national crisis, immigrants and ethnic minorities have been the first and worst victims of civil liberties curtailments. Time

Americans responded to the bombing of Pearl Harbor with a wave of anti-Japanese sentiment. Similarly, 2001 and 2002 saw an increase in anti-Muslim violence in the United States.

and again, when Americans have felt threatened, they have projected their fear and anger onto foreign-born or foreign-looking individuals living in the United States.

In the immediate aftermath of the September 11 terrorist attacks, the Council on American-Islamic Relations (CAIR)

confirmed six hundred reports of anti-Muslim violence, vandalism, and harassment. For example, Muslims in California discovered what appeared to be pig blood thrown on the door of a mosque (a great insult because Islam holds that pigs are unclean), and shots were fired at an Islamic center in Irving, Texas. One man suspected of being Muslim, Balbir Singh Sodhi, an Indian-born father of five, was shot to death at the Phoenix gas station he owned by a man who yelled "I stand for America all the way"[89] as he was arrested by police. Fortunately, violence and hate crimes quickly tapered off within a month or so, but even discounting the six hundred incidents immediately following September 11, the CAIR confirmed a 15 percent increase in reports of anti-Muslim violence from 2001 to 2002. Additionally,

less obvious forms of discrimination persisted: In the first fifteen months after September 11, the federal Equal Employment Opportunity Commission received over seven hundred complaints of employment discrimination from Muslims, Arab Americans, and South Asians.

These incidents show that xenophobia and discrimination are still a reality in the United States. Nevertheless, the initial phases of the war on terrorism also offer hope that Americans have begun to put such tendencies behind them. "One area where

Many Arab Americans, like this San Francisco man whose grocery store was vandalized, were victims of violent acts of xenophobia.

America—government and people—has vastly improved on its past is in its treatment of a threatened minority during war," [90] writes *Newsweek*'s Fareed Zakaria. Almost immediately after the September 11 attacks, national leaders, from New York's Mayor Rudolph Giuliani to President Bush, issued calls for tolerance and asked people not to vent their anger on Muslims or Arab Americans. "America counts millions of Muslims amongst our citizens, and Muslims make an incredibly valuable contribution to our country," said President Bush in a September 17, 2001 address. "In our

New York mayor Rudolph Giuliani called for tolerance in the treatment of all U.S. citizens after the September 11 attacks.

anger and emotion, our fellow Americans must treat each other with respect. . . . Those who feel like they can intimidate our fellow citizens to take out their anger don't represent the best of America, they represent the worst of humankind, and they should be ashamed of that kind of behavior."[91] Bush's comments reflect most Americans' belief that discrimination based on religion or ethnicity is wrong.

The Debate over Ethnic Profiling

With regard to homeland security, the possibility of discrimination arises most obviously in the use of profiling by law enforcement. Profiling is a technique wherein law enforcement officials use what they know about a criminal to narrow down the field of potential suspects. For example, if witnesses report that two young white men robbed a convenience store, the police would concentrate their resources on stopping and questioning young white men in the area rather than nonwhites, women, or older men.

Profiling creates civil liberties concerns when law enforcement agents apply it in too broad a manner, using one characteristic, such as race, as the sole factor in deciding who is a suspect. The most commonly cited example of racial profiling is the practice of police targeting blacks for traffic stops because the police believe that blacks are more likely to be engaged in criminal activity than whites. This practice has been declared illegal by the Supreme Court because overreliance on one factor—in this case race—violates the equal protection clause of the Constitution, which states that the government must apply the law equally and may not give preference to one group of citizens over another.

Similarly, it is illegal for airport security workers to single out an individual to be searched based solely on the fact that he or she is a Muslim or of Arab descent (since terrorists today are most likely to fit those characteristics). Federal aviation regulations state that "an air carrier . . . may not subject a person in air transportation to discrimination on the basis of race, color, national origin, religion, sex, or ancestry."[92] U.S. secretary of transportation Norman Mineta, a Japanese American who was himself interned during World War II, has affirmed his department's opposition to ethnic profiling, declaring that "all of us will face heightened security in the aftermath of September 11, but the security and scrutiny must never become pretexts for unlawful discrimination."[93]

Random Searches and Strained Resources

Instead, all major airports use a system (which was implemented before September 11) called the Computer Assisted Passenger Pre-Screening System (CAPPS). CAPPS is a computer program that uses information about passengers to screen for indicators that suggest whether they may have ties to terrorism or other criminal activities. In part

Ethnic Profiling: A Complex Issue

The line between justified and unjustified ethnic profiling can often be difficult to determine, as authors David Cole and James Dempsey discuss in their book Terrorism and the Constitution.

"The ethnic profiling issue is complicated in the wake of September 11 attacks by the fact that some use of ethnicity is probably permissible. When a bank reports a robbery, and describes the robbers as three white men in their thirties wearing blue shirts, the police can rely on race in seeking to identify and catch the suspects. In that setting, the use of race does not carry any negative stereotypes connotations, but is simply an identifying marker, like the fact that they were wearing blue shirts. . . . Ethnic profiling, by contrast, consists of the reliance on race as a generalization about future behavior. . . . Such reliance on generalizations is probably always impermissible, whereas reliance on race as an identifying criterion is usually permissible.

In the aftermath of September 11, it was often difficult to separate out these two uses of ethnicity. If law enforcement agents had reason to believe there were others involved in the planning and carrying out of the attacks or that their associates might have been planning further attacks, and that these others were Arab or Muslim men, then relying on ethnic criteria to identify guilty parties may have been permissible. . . .

[However,] the use of an ethnic identifying factor becomes more objectionable when it is applied on a nationwide basis over an extended period of time. It is one thing to say that the police, having only the information that three white men robbed a bank, question all white men in the vicinity of the bank immediately after the robbery. It would be another matter for the police nationwide to keep interviewing white males until they find the bank robbers."

because of pressure from civil liberties groups, CAPPS generally does not profile based on national origin, religion, ethnicity, and gender, instead emphasizing indicators such as whether a passenger buys a one-way ticket or pays with cash rather than a credit card. CAPPS also randomly selects some passengers for search, so that individuals trying to evade detection by fitting a low-threat profile may still be searched.

Before September 11, CAPPS only profiled passengers who checked their bags, which meant that 40 to 80 percent of passengers were not profiled. After September 11, CAPPS profiling was extended to all passengers, and the resulting enormous increase in the number of people being searched strained airport security and made for large delays at the airport.

While no one contends that airport security is perfect, the government's stance on ethnic profiling has been particularly controversial. Critics argue that not including religion, ethnicity, and country of origin in profiling techniques is absurd. "Islamic terrorists will necessarily be Muslims, and probably from the Arab world. Not to profile for these characteristic is simply to ignore the nature of today's terrorism,"[94] writes Richard Lowry of the *National Review*. Lowry contends that if ethnicity and national origin were among the CAPPS criteria, all of the September 11 hijackers probably would have been flagged by airport security. Moreover, critics argue that the government has simply gone too far in its efforts to prevent discrimination. They argue that random searches are performed primarily to defend against charges of ethnic profiling and that these searches waste security resources and therefore diminish security efforts.

"It's time to end the madness of mindless airport searches and institute a prudent, thoughtful system of racial profiling,"[95] writes John Fund of the *Wall Street Journal*.

An airport security guard searches a woman while the contents of her purse are checked. With CAPPS, random passengers are sometimes selected for search.

The critical and legally complex question is whether a profiling system that uses factors such as ethnicity would be unconstitutional. Even many opponents of ethnic profiling say that using ethnicity as one of many factors may be permissible, but they warn that such a system would always be prone to abuse. The federal Transportation Security Administration has announced plans to implement CAPPS II, a new profiling system that will take many additional screening factors into account. However, CAPPS II will not be implemented for several years. (Complicating matters, CAPPS II has come under fire from privacy groups because it uses data mining techniques similar to those used in the Terrorism Information Awareness project.)

Targeting Immigrants

While discrimination against Muslims and Arab Americans has received considerable attention, many civil libertarians feel that the government's treatment of immigrants, both legal and illegal, is a much greater cause for concern. Security measures targeted at immigrants include the roundup and subsequent detention of over seven hundred immigrants in the days after September 11; the deportation of thousands of immigrants for minor violations of immigration law; the closing of immigration hearings to the public; and the expansion, under the USA PATRIOT Act, of the attorney general's power to detain legal immigrants. In addition, as part of the creation of the Department of Homeland

Security (DHS), the federal Immigration and Naturalization Service was dissolved and immigration control duties were transferred to DHS. A report from the National Immigration Forum (NIF) states, "This reorganization is a powerful signal that all immigrants will now be viewed as terrorist threats."[96]

The government's focus on immigrants in the war on terrorism is understandable. All nineteen of the September 11 hijackers were immigrants, and fifteen of them were in the United States on expired visas. Many politicians argue that September 11 demonstrated the need to strictly enforce immigration laws. "It is now imperative that we better monitor who we admit into this country, and insure that people honor the terms of their admission," states former Colorado governor Richard Lamm. "We must monitor whom we admit, where they are, whether they are going to the schools they were admitted to attend, and we must know when they leave or don't leave. . . . We must better protect ourselves against illegal immigration so we can better protect ourselves against terrorists."[97]

Critics, however, note that the new security measures have been directed mostly at immigrants from Middle Eastern countries. Civil libertarians are concerned that the government is targeting immigrants based on their ethnicity. According to a report from the Migration Policy Institute (MPI),

Rather than relying on individualized suspicion or intelligence-driven crite-

Immigrants register with the Immigration and Naturalization Service in early 2002. After the terrorist attacks, the INS became part of the Department of Homeland Security.

ria, the government has used national origin as a proxy for evidence of dangerousness. By targeting specific ethnic groups with its new measures, the government has violated [a] core principle of American justice: the Fifth Amendment guarantee of equal protection.[98]

Immigrants-rights advocates say that if the government were selectively applying certain laws to citizens in this manner,

Government Actions Targeting Immigrants in the Weeks After September 11

The following time line provides a brief overview of the government's efforts to investigate immigrants and enforce immigration laws in the weeks after September 11.

September 11–18, 2001: Law enforcement officials detain over seven hundred noncitizens on immigration charges.

September 20, 2001: The Department of Justice issues a temporary order allowing the detention of noncitizens without charge for forty-eight hours (or an additional "reasonable period of time") in the event of emergency.

September 21, 2001: The Department of Justice instructs immigration judges to keep September 11–related bond and deportation hearings closed, allowing no visitors, family, or press and releasing no records or information about the cases.

October 26, 2001: The USA PATRIOT Act becomes law. Among its provisions is a section empowering the attorney general

to order the detainment of any immigrant believed to pose a threat to national security.

October 31, 2001: Attorney General Ashcroft issues an edict allowing the detainment of immigrants even after an immigration judge has ordered their release for lack of evidence. The measure, in effect, results in indefinite detention.

November 9, 2001: The Department of Justice asks five thousand male immigrants from Arab countries to report for voluntary questioning.

November 13, 2001: President Bush issues an executive order permitting noncitizens accused of terrorist activity to be tried in secret military tribunals rather than normal civilian courts.

November 16, 2001: The Department of Justice announces that it will not disclose the identities of immigrants being detained.

there would be a public outcry against such discrimination, but because mostly noncitizens have been targeted, the public has ignored it.

Mass Roundups, Detentions, and Deportations

One of the most publicized and controversial actions that the government took

in the days after September 11 was to detain over seven hundred noncitizens for violations of immigration laws such as staying in the United States beyond the date that their visa expires. Many of those detained were soon released, and none was charged with any terrorism-related crime. But the FBI ordered that more than one hundred detainees would be held without the possibility of bond until they could be completely cleared of any connection to terrorist activity. This process took an average of over two months, and in some cases more than eight months. During this time, detainees were subjected to harsh living conditions and their names were not released to the public.

Civil libertarians object to the secrecy as well as the manner in which the detainees were rounded up, arguing that in relying mostly on ethnicity and country of origin, the government engaged in discriminatory profiling. "There is considerable evidence," notes a report from the Center for Constitutional Rights, "that detainees have been singled out on the basis of their racial and ethnic backgrounds and religious convictions, rather than any specific evidence of wrongdoing."[99] A report from the Department of Justice's Office of the Inspector General supports this charge: "The FBI should have expended more effort attempting to distinguish between aliens who it actually suspected of having a connection to terrorism from those aliens who, while possibly guilty of violating federal immigration law, had no connection to terrorism."[100]

Other civil liberties groups have argued that the detention of immigrants violates the Fifth Amendment guarantee that no person shall "be deprived of life, liberty, or property, without due process of law." Critics say that the detention of persons for two to eight months is out of proportion to the normal course of action for an overstayed visa, and therefore in violation

of the due process clause. The Department of Justice disagrees: "We have done everything within the bounds of our statutory authority," says Jorge Martinez, a department representative. "These individuals have violated our immigration laws, and we have the authority to arrest and detain them—plain and simple."[101]

The mass detentions were only the beginning of a series of government actions targeting immigrants. Section 412 of the USA PATRIOT Act, passed in October 2001, gives the attorney general the authority to detain immigrants, legal or illegal, if there are "reasonable grounds to believe" that they present a threat to national security. The attorney general is not required to share the evidence on which the detention is based.

Then, in June 2002, the Department of Justice announced a special registration program targeted at immigrants from twenty-five Arab and Muslim countries. Noncitizens from those countries were required to submit to being questioned, fingerprinted, and photographed by April 2003. Critics questioned why any immigrant with ties to terrorism would comply with the program, but government officials say that the program uncovered eleven individuals with such ties, out of the more than eighty thousand immigrants who came forward. More troubling for immigrants-rights advocates is that thirteen thousand of those who came forward were marked for deportation for violations of immigration laws. Critics say that the deportations are punishing immigrants who have complied with the law. "People did register out of their good conscience, because they wanted to follow the rules, respect the law," says Fayiz Rahman of the American Muslim Council; he contends that the real goal of the registration program was to "reduce the number of Muslims on American soil."[102] In response to charges of discrimination, DHS officials have said that the registra-

tion of Arab immigrants was only the first phase of a broader program and that eventually immigrants from other countries will also be required to register.

The Rights of Immigrants

The various government actions affecting immigrants in the war on terrorism raise the question of what civil liberties protections immigrants are entitled to. America's

Working with Immigrant Communities

In its report "Immigrants in the Crosshairs: The Quiet Backlash Against America's Immigrants and Refugees," the National Immigration Forum argues that immigrant communities could be valuable intelligence resources in the war on terrorism, but that current policies have made immigrants afraid to come in contact with law enforcement officials.

"There are things the government could do that would greatly assist its ability to collect intelligence within the U.S. Using the increasingly popular tactic of community policing, police departments across the country could redouble their efforts to build trust in immigrant communities. By establishing good relations with communities of the foreign born, the police will be in a better position to collect useful bits of intelligence that might prevent future acts of terrorism. An overhaul of our immigration laws would also increase opportunities to gain intelligence on those already inside the

U.S. Providing opportunities for undocumented immigrants to step out of the shadows and gain legal status, in exchange for making themselves known, would significantly shrink the haystack within which the needle of terrorism hides. . . .

On this score, government actions have hindered, rather than helped, the fight against terrorism. . . . The government seems to have come under the influence of those who would treat all immigrants as terrorists. The cumulative effect of a series of government actions at all levels has created a siege atmosphere in immigrant communities, particularly those of Middle Eastern descent. . . .

Instead of looking for the needle in the haystack, the government has added bale after bale of hay to that haystack. If the goal is finding and rooting out potential terrorists among us, many of the initiatives launched in recent months can only be counterproductive."

history of curtailing the rights of immigrants in times of crisis suggests that Americans may believe that noncitizens enjoy few constitutional protections. But the Supreme Court, in its 1896 decision in *Wong v. United States,* ruled that immigrants as well as citizens are protected by the Bill of Rights. More recently, the Court ruled in the 2001 case *Zafvydas v. Davis* that although illegal immigrants are subject to deportation, they are entitled to due process and equal treatment under the law in deportation proceedings. The Department of Justice's decision in September 2001 to close immigration hearings to the public—excluding even family members and the press—may therefore be unconstitutional.

The United States is engaged in a war on terrorism, and effective homeland security measures cannot ignore the fact that terrorists today are most likely to be Muslim, foreign-born, and of Arab descent. But this fact does not justify discrimination. Whether the issue is airport security or the enforcement of immigration policies, the Constitution requires that laws be applied with regard to individuals' unique circumstances and not just their membership in a larger group.

Chapter Six

Treatment of Suspected Terrorists

Terrorism has both criminal and military aspects, and a central issue in the war on terrorism is whether terrorist acts should be treated as crimes or as acts of war. "Legally speaking," writes Bruce Tucker Smith, an administrative law judge, "the definition of terrorism lies somewhere in the murky half-light between war and crime. Either appellation fits, but neither suits."[103] On the one hand, terrorist acts involve violence and murder, and are clearly illegal. In addition, law enforcement agencies do not want to elevate terrorists to the status of soldiers, choosing instead to characterize them as criminals. On the other hand, some terrorist groups have the organization, sophistication, and capacity for violence of a military force. Moreover, when committed by terrorists, violence and mass murder are more than simply heinous criminal acts; they are the

means by which terrorists try to harm the United States as a nation, and therefore they have national security implications.

Whether terrorism is regarded as a criminal or military act has enormous implications for how suspected terrorists should be treated by the U.S. government. The U.S. criminal justice system affords criminals many civil liberties protections, including the right to trial by jury, access to legal representation, a presumption of innocence, and the requirement that guilt be proven beyond a reasonable doubt. The rules for dealing with spies, saboteurs, and other threats to national security, in contrast, are much less rigid, essentially curtailing the civil liberties of the accused because of the great security threat that he or she may pose.

President Bush and other U.S. leaders have made it clear that the

United States will treat suspected terrorists as national security threats rather than ordinary criminals. "Foreign terrorists who commit war crimes against the United States, in my judgment, are not entitled to and do not deserve the protections of the American Constitution," [104] said Attorney General John Ashcroft in November 2001. This opinion has led to a variety of debates over the extent to which civil liberties concerns should impede the government's efforts to detain, interrogate, and try suspected terrorists. In the first two years of the war on terrorism, there have been more questions than answers on these issues.

Detention Without Trial

An aura of secrecy pervades the detention of suspected terrorists. Journalist Mark Bowden reports that "there is no clear count of suspected terrorists now in U.S. custody." [105] As of July 2003, about 680 people were being held at a specially constructed prison at the U.S. naval base in Guantánamo Bay, Cuba. Most of them were captured during the U.S. invasion of Afghanistan in October 2001. Hundreds of other suspects are being held around the world in America's military installations or those of its allies. The government has not made public the numbers or names of those being held for intelligence reasons: "Once a top-level suspect is publicly known to be in

custody," reports Bowden, "his intelligence value falls. His organization scatters, altering its plans, disguises, cover stories, codes, tactics, and communication methods." [106]

Of course, civil libertarians and human rights advocates object whenever any government secretly arrests people and holds them without charging them with a crime.

Suspected terrorists captured during the U.S. invasion of Afghanistan are detained at Camp X-Ray at Guantánamo Bay, Cuba.

As law professor Stephen Schulhofer puts it, "To say that the Executive Branch on its own determination can pick somebody up and hold them indefinitely without any procedure or access to a court or to counsel or the press is an absolutely staggering thought." [107] However, civil libertarians understand the intelligence concerns involved, and many of them accept the need for secrecy in the detention of suspected terrorists. Moreover, in the absence of more information about those being held by the government and how they are being treated, even the most mistrustful government watchdog groups have little choice but to hope that the U.S. government conducts this aspect of the war on terrorism in a fair and lawful manner. For example, they must accept Secretary of Defense Donald Rumsfeld's assurance that "no detainee has been harmed; no detainee has been mistreated in any way." [108]

However, the issue of detention without trial came closer to home with the arrest of two U.S. citizens with ties to the al-Qaeda terrorist network. Yaser Esam

The Importance of Public Trials

One of civil libertarians' main concerns about the government's treatment of suspected terrorists is that they will be tried in secret. The most commonly cited benefit of public trials is that they help ensure that the accused get a fair trial. In the June 10, 2002, issue of the Nation, *attorney Edward J. Klaris discusses how the public also benefits from public trials.*

"Public criminal trials are so commonplace in our society that few think twice about the rights underlying this openness. When they do, the criminal defendant's Sixth Amendment right to a public trial usually comes to mind. However, it is now beyond dispute that a separate right of access to attend trials also arises from the First Amendment. That right to attend criminal proceedings—which belongs to the press and public, not to the defendants—mandates that trials be open, absent compelling and clearly articulated reasons for closing them. This independent constitutional right of access was first recognized by the Supreme Court in 1980 in *Richmond Newspapers v. Virginia.* In that case, the Court held that an order closing the courtroom for the trial was unconstitutional, noting the public policy reasons behind the rule: 'When a shocking crime occurs, a community reaction of outrage and public protest often follows, and thereafter the open processes of justice serve an important prophylactic [preventive] purpose, providing an outlet for community concern, hostility, and emotion.' In describing the need for open criminal proceedings, Professor Laurence Tribe of Harvard Law School wrote: 'The courthouse is a 'theatre of justice,' wherein a vital social drama is staged; if its doors are locked, the public can only wonder whether the solemn ritual of communal condemnation has been properly performed.'"

Secretary of Defense Donald Rumsfeld assures the American public that no alleged terrorists detained by the U.S. government have been mistreated.

Hamdi, born in Louisiana to Saudi Arabian parents, was captured while fighting for the Taliban in Afghanistan, and Jose Padilla (also known as Abdullah al-Mujahir), a New Yorker of Puerto Rican ancestry, was arrested in June 2001 at a Chicago airport after allegedly plotting a bombing with al-Qaeda operatives. Like the hundreds of foreign terror suspects, neither man was charged with a crime, but both have been held in military brigs since their arrests.

Unlawful Combatants

In legal terms, the Bush administration has justified its detention without charge of terror suspects, including Hamdi and Padilla, by declaring that they are "unlawful combatants." This term comes from the 1949 Geneva Convention, which defines the laws and customs of modern war, particularly the treatment of individuals captured during wartime. The Geneva Convention distinguishes between captured lawful combatants, or prisoners of war (POWs), and unlawful combatants. Unlawful combatants are those who do not carry their arms openly, do not wear a uniform or insignia to identify themselves as soldiers, and otherwise conceal their identities before launching an attack. Unlawful combatants do not enjoy the same privileges as POWs, who, according to the Geneva Convention, have the right to refuse to disclose military information and cannot be held indefinitely but must instead be tried or freed once hostilities are over.

Secretary of Defense Donald Rumsfeld and other U.S. officials have said that since terrorist groups such as al-Qaeda are not recognized military forces and since they do not follow the rules of war, terrorists are unlawful combatants and may be held

Suspected terrorist Yaser Esam Hamdi is led to an Afghanistan prison following his capture. Hamdi has been labeled an "unlawful combatant" and was detained without officially being charged with a crime.

indefinitely without trial. Former Supreme Court justice nominee Robert Bork defends this reasoning:

> The government's policy is as follows: if a captured unlawful enemy combatant is believed to have further information about terrorism, he can be held without access to legal counsel and without charges being filed. Once the government is satisfied that it has all the relevant information it can obtain, the captive can be held until the end of hostilities, or be released, or be brought up on charges before a criminal court. [109]

Civil libertarians are concerned that by simply labeling someone as an unlawful combatant, the United States is claiming authority to hold terror suspects indefinitely, in violation of the Fifth Amendment's guarantee of due process and the Sixth Amendment's guarantee of a speedy and public trial. They point out that in the war on terrorism, it is unclear when, if ever, "hostilities" will end. In addition, they maintain that the designation of terror suspects as unlawful combatants is unconstitutional because the United States has made no formal declaration of war, which requires an act of Congress. The Constitution, argues the American Civil Liberties Union (ACLU), gives Congress, not the president, "the power to declare war, make rules concerning captures, and regulate the armed forces." [110] Finally, civil libertarians worry that labeling terror suspects as unlawful combatants is part of a broader plan to try terror suspects in military tribunals rather than normal courts of law.

Military Tribunals

President Bush first raised the issue of military tribunals on November 13, 2001, when he issued an executive order stating that noncitizens accused of terrorism could be tried under a military tribunal. With the designation of terror suspects Hamdi and Padillo as unlawful combatants, there is

speculation that military tribunals could be used to try both citizens and noncitizens.

Military tribunals are a little-known aspect of the U.S. justice system; in the first two years of the war on terrorism, no one has been tried on terrorist charges outside of normal federal court. Military tribunals are different from either normal civilian courts or ordinary military courts-martial. The specific guidelines for military tribunals may be set on a case-by-case basis by the secretary of defense. They will probably be closed to the public and have a

The Need for Clearer Guidelines on Military Tribunals

Although President Bush issued his executive order authorizing military tribunals for terror suspects in November 2001, in the first two years of the war on terrorism no military tribunals have been convened, and the administration has issued only general guidelines on how such tribunals would be conducted. In a December 2001 Atlantic Monthly *article, Stuart Taylor Jr. suggests that more specifics about military tribunals would allay civil libertarian concerns about them.*

"On November 28, Assistant Attorney General Michael Chertoff, head of the criminal division, assured the Senate Judiciary Committee that the detailed rules—to be drawn up by the Pentagon—would contain credible fair-trial guarantees. And a senior Administration official tells me: 'I don't think that we're going to end up using mil-

itary tribunals to try people captured in the United States'—not even accused Al Qaeda terrorists. Not many of them, at least. In addition, this official predicts, if and when military commissions are used, the rules will require a presumption of innocence and proof of guilt beyond a reasonable doubt, even for terrorists caught in Afghanistan. And White House Counsel Alberto R. Gonzales told me that any military proceeding would be public except to the extent necessary to protect 'national security interests.'

These are comforting words. If the President, or Attorney General John D. Ashcroft, or Defense Secretary Donald Rumsfeld publicly provides similar assurances, it would allay the concerns of many of the domestic critics who are alarmed by the breathtaking sweep of the President's order."

lower standard of due process than either civilian courts or military courts-martial. For example, it is likely that guilt will not have to be proved beyond a reasonable doubt, the verdict need not be unanimous, and secondhand hearsay evidence and evidence that has been collected improperly may be allowed. Defendants might not be allowed the lawyer of their choosing or the right to appeal.

Trial by military tribunals is one of the most controversial measures that the Bush administration has proposed in the war on terrorism. "The Administration's proposal to substitute military tribunals for the regular justice system poses a profound challenge to the nation's ability to preserve civil liberties as it combats terrorism," [111] warns the ACLU. Civil libertarians have marshaled an array of arguments opposing the tribunals. The ACLU charges that, like detention of suspects without trial, military tribunals are unconstitutional unless war has formally been declared. Civil liberties groups also argue that, since military tribunals are presided over by military personnel and not independent judges, they concentrate too much power in the executive branch of government. Critics also question why military tribunals are necessary, pointing to the successful prosecution, in federal court, of the terrorists who bombed the World Trade Center in 1993. Above all, human rights advocates worry that, by shrouding proceedings in secrecy and limiting the rights of the accused, the use of military tribunals will lead to the conviction of people who are innocent.

In response, advocates of military tribunals have argued that normal criminal trials are too slow. One of the trials resulting from the 1993 World Trade Center bombing lasted nearly nine months; another involved more than two hundred witnesses; and either one could have resulted in a mistrial if a single juror had refused to join in the verdict. Officials have also expressed concern that such high-profile trials would make tempting targets for other terrorist attacks.

However, the main argument for military tribunals, just as for detention without charge, revolves around intelligence and need for secrecy. Defendants in criminal trials are protected by the Sixth Amendment's guarantee of a public trial. Public trials of terrorists raise the same intelligence problems as public arrests: They may inadvertently give information to other terrorists. The evidence presented in such trials would reveal the extent of the government's intelligence operations for a particular terrorist group. "If the terrorists know what you know, then they'll know how you found it, and they'll shut that channel off," [112] says former federal prosecutor Ruth Wedgewood. Skip Brandon, a former deputy assistant director of intelligence at the Federal Bureau of Investigation, says that "we've had espionage cases that should have been brought [to trial], but we didn't because we couldn't make the case without introducing evidence that would compromise others." [113]

Coercive Interrogation of Suspected Terrorists

Intelligence concerns dominate the civil liberties issues surrounding arrest, detention, and trial, but the area in which intelligence gathering and civil liberties come most clearly into conflict is in the interrogation of suspected terrorists. U.S. officials have repeatedly emphasized the importance of gaining more information on terrorists' whereabouts and plans. The question is, if authorities have captured a member of a terrorist group who refuses to talk, how far should interrogators be allowed to go in order to extract potentially life-saving information from the suspect?

The debate about terrorism and interrogation gained widespread attention in November 2001 when Harvard law professor Alan Dershowitz published an article in the *Los Angeles Times* suggesting that the physical torture of terror suspects might be justified in very narrow circumstances. Dershowitz proposed a situation in which a captured terrorist knows of an imminent large-scale threat, such as a ticking bomb set to explode at a certain time, but refuses to disclose the details necessary to prevent the attack. "Would torturing one guilty terrorist to prevent the deaths of a thousand innocent civilians shock the conscience of all decent people?"[114] asks Dershowitz.

Dershowitz's example, although both hypothetical and extreme, raises the classic ethics question of whether the ends justify the means. He maintains that in such an extreme case, law enforcement agents should torture the suspect for information in order to prevent the terrorist's bomb from going off. Dershowitz maintains that in the war on terrorism, the legal system should prepare for such extreme cases, authorizing courts to issue "torture warrants" when doing so is the only way to

Harvard law professor Alan Dershowitz advocates the use of torture in cases in which a suspected terrorist has information that could save lives.

save lives. His conclusion is that if torture is going to occur, it should be subject to judicial oversight.

Dershowitz's proposal that the United States condone torture outraged many civil liberties and human rights groups that have been campaigning for the elimination of torture in other countries for decades. Philosophers dissected the do-the-ends-justify-the-means questions that Dershowitz posed, and legal scholars pointed out the constitutional obstacles to his proposal. The Eighth Amendment, of course, protects against "cruel and unusual punishments"; more generally, most constitutional scholars believe that an individual's right of bodily integrity is implicit in the Bill of Rights. In the realm of international law, the Geneva Convention completely bans the mistreatment of prisoners. Finally, President Bush has made America's stance toward torture quite clear: "The United States is committed to the worldwide elimination of torture and we are leading this fight by example,"[115] he declared on June 26, 2003, the United Nations's day to honor torture victims.

Ideals vs. Reality

Nevertheless, the issue of interrogating terror suspects remains a delicate one, with many gray areas. As journalist Mark

Conducting Coercive Interrogation on Foreign Soil

Hundreds of terror suspects are being held not by the United States, but by its allies in the war on terrorism. Many of these countries have much less restrictive laws governing the treatment of criminals, and some people believe that these suspects have been subjected to interrogation tactics that are illegal in the United States. Reporters Rajiv Chandrasekaran and Peter Finn note in this excerpt from a March 2002 Washington Post *article:*

"Since Sept. 11, the U.S. government has secretly transported dozens of people suspected of links to terrorists to countries other than the United States, bypassing extradition procedures and legal formalities, according to Western diplomats and intelligence sources. The suspects have been taken to countries, including Egypt and Jordan, whose intelligence services have close ties to the CIA [Central Intelligence Agency] and where they can be subjected to interrogation tactics—including torture and threats to families—that are illegal in the United States, the sources said. In some cases, U.S. intelligence agents remain closely involved in the interrogation, the sources said.

'After September 11, these sorts of movements have been occurring all the time,' a U.S. diplomat said. 'It allows us to get information from terrorists in a way we can't do on U.S. soil.'"

Bowden explains, interrogators do not necessarily need to physically torture suspects to get them to talk:

> There are methods that, some people argue, fall short of torture. Called "torture lite," these include sleep deprivation, exposure to heat or cold, the use of drugs to cause confusion, rough treatment (slapping, shoving, or shaking), forcing a prisoner to stand for days at a time or to sit in uncomfortable positions, and playing on his fears for himself and his family. Although excruciating for the victim, these tactics generally leave no permanent marks and do not do lasting physical harm. [116]

In 1987, Israel legalized some of these forms of coercive interrogation, permitting "moderate physical pressure" and "nonviolent psychological pressure" in cases where the suspect had information that could prevent terror attacks. In 1999, however, the Israeli Supreme Court banned even these techniques, in part because their use had become much more widespread than originally intended. Israel's experience is often cited as a case study in how even "torture lite" can be overused and abused. Nevertheless, Bowden is not alone in speculating that some of these interrogation techniques are being used on some of the hundreds of terror suspects being held around the world by the United States and its allies in the war on terrorism.

The debate over coercive interrogation essentially pits decent people's belief that torture is immoral against their urge to do whatever is necessary to stop terrorists. In this respect, it mirrors many of the debates over civil liberties in the war on terrorism. Again and again the questions come down to whether an open and democratic society must resort to undemocratic curtailments of liberty in order to prevent terrorism.

Notes

Introduction: Liberty vs. Security: A Necessary Trade-Off?

1. George W. Bush, "Address to a Joint Session of Congress and the American People," September 20, 2001. www.whitehouse.gov.
2. Alan M. Dershowitz, *Why Terrorism Works: Understanding the Threat, Responding to the Challenge.* New Haven, CT: Yale University Press, 2002, p. 106.
3. Quoted in Thomas F. Powers, "Can We Be Secure and Free?" *Public Interest,* Spring 2003, p. 3.
4. Anthony D. Romero, "In Defense of Liberty: Accountability and Responsiveness to Civil Liberties," *Vital Speeches of the Day,* January 1, 2002, p. 169.
5. Gene Stephens, "Can We Be Safe and Free?" *USA Today,* January 2003.
6. Richard Posner, "Security Versus Civil Liberties," *Atlantic Monthly,* December 2001, p. 48.
7. American Civil Liberties Union, *The USA PATRIOT ACT and Government Actions That Threaten Our Civil Liberties.* www.aclu.org.
8. Quoted in Alisa Solomon, "The Big Chill," *Nation,* June 2, 2003, p. 17.
9. Quoted in *BusinessWeek,* "Security vs. Civil Liberties," October 1, 2001, p. 50.
10. Quoted in Charles Lane, "Debate Crystallizes on War, Rights," *Washington Post,* September 2, 2002.
11. John Ashcroft, "Securing Our Liberty: How America Is Winning the War on Terror," speech before the American Enterprise Institute, August 19, 2003. www.aei.org.
12. Lawyers Committee for Human Rights, "Imbalance of Powers: How Changes to U.S. Law & Policy Since 9/11 Erode Human Rights and Civil Liberties," September 2002– March 2003. www.lchr.org.
13. David Cole and James X. Dempsey, *Terrorism and the Constitution: Sacrificing Civil Liberties in the Name of National Security.* New York: New Press, 2002, p. 15.
14. American Civil Liberties Union, *Insatiable Appetite: The Government's Demand for New and Unnecessary Powers After September 11,* April 2002. www.aclu.org.
15. Quoted in Richard Lacayo, "The War Comes Back Home," *Time,* May 12, 2003, p. 30.

Chapter One: A History of Civil Liberties During Wartime

16. Angie Cannon, "Taking Liberties," *U.S. News & World Report,* May 12, 2003, p. 44.
17. Quoted in Ira Glasser, "More Safe, Less Free: A Short History of Wartime Civil Liberties," in Danny Goldberg, Victor Goldberg, and Robert Greenwald, eds., *It's a Free Country: Personal Freedom in America After September 11.* New York: RDV Books, 2002, p. 11.
18. Glasser, "More Safe, Less Free," p. 14.
19. Geoffrey R. Stone, "Civil Liberties at Risk Again: A U.S. Tradition," *Chicago Tribune,* February 16, 2003.

20. Bruce Watson, "Crackdown! When Bombs Terrorized America, the Attorney General Launched the 'Palmer Raids,'" *Smithsonian,* February 2002, p. 50.

21. Quoted in Watson, "Crackdown!" p. 51.

22. American Civil Liberties Union, *Civil Liberties After 9/11: The ACLU Defends Freedom.* www.aclu.org.

23. Quoted in *NOW: With Bill Moyers* website. "Civil Liberties After 9/11: Timeline." www.pbs.org.

24. Glasser, "More Safe, Less Free," p. 17.

25. Stuart Taylor Jr., "Rights, Liberties, and Security: Recalibrating the Balance After September 11," *Brookings Review,* Winter 2003, p. 25.

26. Jay Winik, "Security Before Liberty: Today's Curbs on Freedom Are Nothing Compared with Earlier Wars," *Opinion Journal.com,* October 23, 2001. www.opinionjournal.com.

27. Laurence H. Tribe, "We Can Strike a Balance on Civil Liberties," *Wall Street Journal,* September 27, 2001.

28. Daniel Hellinger, "Taking Liberties with the Constitution," *Synthesis/Regeneration,* Spring 2002, p. 5.

29. Stone, "Civil Liberties at Risk Again," p. 1.

Chapter Two: Patriotism and the First Amendment

30. Eric Foner, "The Most Patriotic Act," *Nation,* October 8, 2001, p. 13.

31. Watson, "Crackdown!" p. 50.

32. Quoted in Victor S. Navasky, "Profiled in Cowardice," *Nation,* November 5, 2001, p. 23.

33. Quoted in Solomon, "The Big Chill," p. 17.

34. Paul McMasters, "The More We Know, the More Secure We Are," December 7, 2001. www.firstamendmentcenter.org.

35. Foner, "The Most Patriotic Act," p. 13.

36. Bush, "Address to a Joint Session of Congress and the American People."

37. Ciro Scotti, "Politically Incorrect Is Downright American," *Business Week Online,* September 26, 2001. www.businessweek.com.

38. Nancy Chang, *The USA Patriot Act: What's So Patriotic About Trampling the Bill of Rights?* Center for Constitutional Rights, November 2001. www.ccr-ny.org.

39. American Civil Liberties Union, "Section 215 FAQ," October 24, 2002. www.aclu.org.

40. Paul McMasters, "The War on Journalism," October 22, 2001. www.firstamendmentcenter.org.

41. Quoted in Laura Parker, Kevin Johnson, and Toni Locy, "Secure Often Means Secret," *USA Today,* May 16, 2002, p. 1A.

42. Lawyers Committee for Human Rights, "Imbalance of Powers."

43. Ken Paulson, "A Matter of Balance: Secrecy Doesn't Guarantee Security," March 24, 2002. www.firstamendmentcenter.org.

44. Quoted in Gina Barton, "Patriotism and the News: How 'American' Should the American Press Be?" *Quill Magazine,* December 2001, p. 20.

45. Quoted in Bob Edwards, "The Press and Freedom," *Neiman Reports,* Summer 2003, p. 82.

46. Edwards, "The Press and Freedom," p. 82.

47. Dennis Pluchinsky, "They Heard It All Here, and That's the Trouble," *Washington Post,* June 16, 2002.

48. Ken Paulson, "A Patriotic Press Is a Vigilant One," September 23, 2001. www.freedomforum.org.

49. First Amendment Center, *State of the First Amendment 2002,* 2002. www.firstamendmentcenter.org.

Chapter Three: Government Surveillance and the Right to Privacy

50. Quoted in Phillip Taylor, "Summary of the Right to Privacy." www.freedomforum.org.

51. Joseph Atick, "Surveillance Technology: Tracking Terrorists and Protecting Public Places," *IEEE Spectrum Online*, October 31, 2001. www.spectrum.ieee.org.

52. Dershowitz, *Why Terrorism Works*, p. 204.

53. American Civil Liberties Union, "Q & A on Face-Recognition," September 2, 2003. www.aclu.org.

54. American Civil Liberties Union, "The Four Problems with Public Video Surveillance," May 22, 2003. www.aclu.org.

55. Sonia Arrison, "Symposium: Will the Government's Use of Biometrics Endanger Civil Liberties? Yes: Loss of Freedoms Tend to Happen Incrementally Rather than Immediately," *Insight on the News*, February 25, 2002, p. 40.

56. David Kopel and Michael Krause, "Face the Facts: Facial Recognition Technology's Troubled Past—and Troubling Future," *Reason*, October 2002, p. 26.

57. Libby Tucker, "Gotcha!" *Science World*, March 7, 2003, p. 16.

58. Marti Dinerstein, "IDs for Illegals: The 'Matricula Consular' Advances Mexico's Immigration Agenda," January 2003. www.cis.org.

59. *Government Computer News*, "To End ID Crime," October 21, 2002, p. S12.

60. James Glassman, "Time for a National ID Card?" November 4, 2001. www.aei.org.

61. Quoted in Barbara Dority, "Halt and Show Your Papers!" *Humanist*, March/April 2002, p. 10.

62. Clyde Wayne Crews Jr., "Human Bar Code," November 1, 2002. www.cato.org.

63. Randall Stross, "Counterfeit Freedom," *U.S. News & World Report*, October 8, 2001, p. 43.

64. Alan Dershowitz, "Why Fear National ID Cards?" *New York Times*, October 13, 2001.

65. Steven Levy, "Playing the ID Card," *Newsweek*, May 13, 2002, p. 44.

66. Quoted in Levy, "Playing the ID Card," p. 44.

67. Levy, "Playing the ID Card," p. 44.

68. American Civil Liberties Union, "Q & A on the Pentagon's 'Total Information Awareness' Program," April 20, 2003. www.aclu.org.

69. William Safire, "You Are a Suspect," *New York Times*, November 14, 2002.

70. James Harper, "Symposium. Q: Should the White House Expand the 'Total Information Awareness' Project? No: These Databases Pose More of a Threat to Ordinary Citizens than to Terrorists," *Insight on the News*, December 24, 2002, p. 46.

71. Stuart Taylor Jr., "How Civil-Liberty Hysteria May Endanger Us All," *National Journal*, February 22, 2003.

72. Solveig Singleton, "Symposium: Q: Will the Government's Use of Biometrics Endanger American Civil Liberties? No: Authoritarianism Is Not a Gadget, It's a State of Mind," *Insight on the News*, February 25, 2002, p. 40.

Chapter Four: The PATRIOT Act and the Fourth Amendment

73. Center for Constitutional Rights, *The State of Civil Liberties: One Year Later: Erosion of Civil Liberties in the Post 9/11 Era*. Center for Constitutional Rights, September 2002. www.ccr-ny.org.

74. Brendan Miniter, "Truth and Justice," *OpinionJournal.com*, August 26, 2002. www.opinionjournal.com.

75. Mark Reibling, "Uncuff the FBI," *Opinion Journal.com,* June 4, 2002. www.opinion journal.com.

76. John Ashcroft, press conference, October 18, 2001. www.usdoj.gov.

77. Robert Levy, "Assaults on Liberty," Cato Institute, November 24, 2002. www.cato. org.

78. Ashcroft, press conference.

79. Chang, *The USA Patriot Act.*

80. Dahlia Lithwick and Julia Turner, "A Guide to the Patriot Act, Part 4," *Slate.com,* September 11, 2003. http://slate.msn. com.

81. Lithwick and Turner, "A Guide to the Patriot Act."

82. George W. Bush, speech before the FBI Academy, Quantico, Virginia, September 10, 2003. www.whitehouse.gov.

83. Ashcroft, "Securing Our Liberty."

84. Quoted in Preserving Life & Liberty, "Stories and Articles." www.lifeandliberty. gov.

85. Quoted in Preserving Life and Liberty "Stories and Articles."

86. Chang, *The USA Patriot Act.*

87. Quoted in Amy Goldstein, "Fierce Fight over Secrecy, Scope of Law," *Washington Post,* September 8, 2003.

Chapter Five: Discrimination Against Minorities and Immigrants

88. Quoted in Digital History, "Interpreting Primary Sources: World War I." www. digitalhistory.uh.edu.

89. Quoted in Vintage Foster, "Protect Diversity, a Way of Life," *Dallas Business Journal,* October 12, 2001.

90. Fareed Zakaria, "Freedom vs. Security: Delicate Balance," *Newsweek,* July 8, 2002, p. 26.

91. George W. Bush, remarks at the Islamic Center of Washington, D.C., September 17, 2001. www.whitehouse.gov.

92. Quoted in Sasha Polakow-Suransky, "Flying While Brown," *American Prospect,* November 19, 2001, p. 14.

93. Quoted in Polakow-Suransky, "Flying While Brown," p. 14.

94. Richard Lowry, "Profiles in Cowardice: How to Deal with the Terrorist Threat— and How Not To," *National Review,* January 28, 2002, p. 12.

95. John Fund, "Willful Ignorance," *Opinion Journal.com,* May 22, 2002. www.opinion journal.com.

96. National Immigration Forum, "Immigrants in the Crosshairs: The Quiet Backlash Against America's Immigrants and Refugees," *National Immigration Forum Backgrounder,* December 16, 2002. www.immigrationforum.org.

97. Richard Lamm, "Terrorism and Immigration: We Need a Border," *Vital Speeches of the Day,* March 1, 2002, p. 298.

98. Muzaffer A. Chishti et al., *America's Challenge: Domestic Security, Civil Liberties, and National Unity After September 11.* Washington, DC: Migration Policy Institute, 2003. www.migrationpolicy.org.

99. Center for Constitutional Rights, *The State of Civil Liberties,* p. 12.

100. Department of Justice Office of the Inspector General, "Department of Justice Inspector General Issues Report on Treatment of Aliens Held on Immigration Charges in Connection with the Investigation of the September 11 Terrorist Attacks," June 2, 2003. www.usdoj.gov.

101. Quoted in Rui Kaneya, "Immigrants Swept Up in Security Debate," *Chicago Reporter,* January 2003, p. 3.

102. Quoted in *Europe Intelligence Wire*, "13,000 Arab and Muslim Men Face Deportation from US," June 7, 2003.

Chapter Six: Treatment of Suspected Terrorists

103. Bruce Tucker Smith, "Symposium. Q: Are U.S. Military Tribunals Appropriate for Dealing with Suspected Terrorists? Yes: Such Tribunals Will Ensure That the Dictates of Both Fairness and National Security Are Met," *Insight on the News*, January 28, 2002, p. 40.

104. Quoted in Cam Simpson, "Latest Terror Suspects Seen as New Candidates for Military Tribunals," *Knight Ridder/Tribune News Service*, March 18, 2003, p. K6893.

105. Mark Bowden, "The Dark Art of Interrogation," *Atlantic Monthly*, October 2003, p. 54.

106. Bowden, "The Dark Art of Interrogation," p. 54.

107. Quoted in Lacayo, "The War Comes Back Home," p. 30.

108. Quoted in George Edmonson, "War on Terrorism: Detainee Treatment Defended," *Atlanta-Journal Constitution*, January 23, 2002.

109. Robert Bork, "Civil Liberties After 9/11," *Commentary*, July/August 2003, p. 29.

110. American Civil Liberties Union, "Interested Persons Memo on the Indefinite Detention Without Charge of American Citizens as 'Enemy Combatants,'" September 13, 2002. www.aclu.org.

111. American Civil Liberties Union, "Interested Persons Memo on Military Tribunals in Terrorism Cases," November 29, 2001. www.aclu.org.

112. Quoted in Jason Zengerle, "Infinite Justice—Can Courts Try Terrorists?" *New Republic*, November 19, 2001, p. 17.

113. Quoted in Zengerle, "Infinite Justice," p. 17.

114. Alan Dershowitz, "Is There a Torturous Road to Justice?" *Los Angeles Times*, November 8, 2001.

115. Quoted in *Economist*, "The Pledge; Human Rights and Terrorism," July 5, 2003, p. 25.

116. Bowden, "The Dark Art of Interrogation," p. 51.

For Further Reading

Books

Alan Dershowitz, *Shouting Fire: Civil Liberties in a Turbulent Age.* Boston: Little Brown, 2002. In this overview of civil liberties controversies, Harvard law professor Alan Dershowitz discusses topics ranging from TV censorship to the death penalty. Though written before the September 11 attacks, the book includes an entire chapter on the suspension of civil liberties in times of crisis.

Katrina vanden Heuvel, ed., *A Just Response:* The Nation *on Terrorism, Democracy, and September 11, 2001.* New York: Thunder's Mouth Press. This book is an anthology of articles and editorials from the *Nation,* a liberal magazine that is extremely critical of the Bush administration's response to September 11.

Websites

American Civil Liberties Union (ACLU) (www.aclu.org). A national organization that defends Americans' civil rights guaranteed in the U.S. Constitution. Its website offers numerous reports, fact sheets, and policy statements on issues such as the USA PATRIOT Act, government surveillance, military tribunals for terror suspects, and homeland security measures targeted at immigrants.

ANSER Institute for Homeland Security (www.homelandsecurity.org). A nonprofit, nonpartisan think tank that works to educate the public about homeland security issues. The institute's website contains a virtual library of fact sheets, reports, legislation, and government documents and statistics on homeland security issues.

Arab American Institute (AAI) (www.assi usa.org). A nonprofit organization committed to the civic and political empowerment of Americans of Arab descent. Opposes ethnic profiling and the restriction of immigrants' civil liberties in the name of homeland security. Its website provides background information and position statements on a variety of issues.

Cato Institute (www.cato.org). A nonpartisan public policy research foundation dedicated to limiting the role of government and protecting individual liberties. Numerous articles and opinion pieces on topics such as national ID cards, the Terrorism Information Awareness project, and military tribunals for terror suspects are available on the institute's website.

Center for Constitutional Rights (CCR) (www.ccr-ny.org). Dedicated to protecting and advancing the rights guaranteed by the U.S. Constitution and the Universal Declaration of Human Rights. Opposes many of the measures taken by the government since September 11 and has a variety of fact sheets and reports available on its website.

Department of Homeland Security (DHS) (www.dhs.gov). Offers a wide variety of information on homeland security, including press releases, speeches and testimony, and reports on new initiatives in the war on terrorism.

National Immigration Forum (NIF) (www.immigrationforum.org). Advocates public policies that welcome immigrants and refugees and that are fair and supportive to newcomers to the United States. The NIF website offers a special section on immigration in the wake of September 11.

Preserving Life & Liberty (www.lifeandliberty.gov). Set up by the U.S. Department of Justice to address civil libertarians' concerns about the USA PATRIOT Act and other homeland security initiatives. Offers answers to frequently asked questions about the USA PATRIOT Act and testimony from U.S. officials in support of the act.

Terrorism: Questions & Answers (www.terrorismanswers.com). This website, sponsored by the Council on Foreign Relations, provides information on a wide range of terrorism-related issues, including civil liberties issues.

Works Consulted

Books

David Cole and James X. Dempsey, *Terrorism and the Constitution: Sacrificing Civil Liberties in the Name of National Security.* New York: New Press, 2002. Cole and Dempsey provide an overview of how security concerns have been used to curtail civil liberties since the 1980s. In the final chapters of the book, the authors address the war on terrorism, arguing that homeland security measures need not come at the expense of civil liberties.

Alan M. Dershowitz, *Why Terrorism Works: Understanding the Threat, Responding to the Challenge.* New Haven, CT: Yale University Press, 2002. Defense lawyer and law professor Alan Dershowtiz argues in this book that, in the war on terrorism, the United States must strike a new balance between security and freedom, even if that means curtailing some civil liberties.

Danny Goldberg, Victor Goldberg, and Robert Greenwald, eds., *It's a Free Country: Personal Freedom in America After September 11.* New York: RDV Books, 2002. This book is an anthology of opinion essays, congressional testimonies, and personal narratives about civil liberties curtailments in the wake of September 11.

Periodicals

Sonia Arrison, "Symposium: Will the Government's Use of Biometrics Endanger Civil Liberties? Yes: Loss of Freedoms Tend to Happen Incrementally Rather than Immediately," *Insight on the News,* February 25, 2002.

Gina Barton, "Patriotism and the News: How 'American' Should the American Press Be?" *Quill Magazine,* December 2001.

Robert Bork, "Civil Liberties After 9/11," *Commentary,* July/August 2003.

Mark Bowden, "The Dark Art of Interrogation," *Atlantic Monthly,* October 2003.

BusinessWeek, "Security vs. Civil Liberties," October 1, 2001.

Angie Cannon, "Taking Liberties," *U.S. News & World Report,* May 12, 2003.

Rajiv Chandrasekaran and Peter Finn, "U.S. Behind Secret Transfer of Terror Suspects," *Washington Post,* March 11, 2002.

Adam Cohen, "Rough Justice: The Attorney General Has Powerful New Tools to Fight Terrorism. Has He Gone Too Far?" *Time,* December 10, 2001.

David Cole, "Enemy Aliens and American Freedom: Experience Teaches That Whatever the Threat, Certain Principles Remain Sacrosanct," *Nation,* September 23, 2002.

Alan Dershowitz, "Is There a Torturous Road to Justice?" *Los Angeles Times,* November 8, 2001.

———, "Why Fear National ID Cards?" *New York Times,* October 13, 2001.

Barbara Dority, "Halt and Show Your Papers!" *Humanist,* March/April 2002.

Economist, "The Pledge; Human Rights and Terrorism," July 5, 2003.

George Edmonson, "War on Terrorism: Detainee Treatment Defended," *Atlanta-Journal Constitution,* January 23, 2002.

Bob Edwards, "The Press and Freedom," *Neiman Reports,* Summer 2003.

Europe Intelligence Wire, "13,000 Arab and Muslim Men Face Deportation from US," June 7, 2003.

Eric Foner, "The Most Patriotic Act," *Nation,* October 8, 2001.

Vintage Foster, "Protect Diversity, a Way of Life," *Dallas Business Journal,* October 12, 2001.

Susan Gellman, "The First Amendment in Times That Try Men's Souls," *Law and Contemporary Problems,* Spring 2002.

Amy Goldstein, "Fierce Fight over Secrecy, Scope of Law," *Washington Post,* September 8, 2003.

Government Computer News, "To End ID Crime," October 21, 2002.

James Harper, "Symposium. Q: Should the White House Expand the 'Total Information Awareness' Project? No: These Databases Pose More of a Threat to Ordinary Citizens than to Terrorists," *Insight on the News,* December 24, 2002.

Daniel Hellinger, "Taking Liberties with the Constitution," *Synthesis/Regeneration,* Spring 2002.

Rui Kaneya, "Immigrants Swept Up in Security Debate," *Chicago Reporter,* January 2003.

Edward J. Klaris, "Justice Can't Be Done in Secret," *Nation,* June 10, 2002.

David Kopel and Michael Krause, "Face the Facts: Facial Recognition Technology's Troubled Past—and Troubling Future," *Reason,* October 2002.

Richard Lacayo, "The War Comes Back Home," *Time,* May 12, 2003.

Richard Lamm, "Terrorism and Immigration: We Need a Border," *Vital Speeches of the Day,* March 1, 2002.

Charles Lane, "Debate Crystallizes on War, Rights," *Washington Post,* September 2, 2002.

Steven Levy, "Playing the ID Card," *Newsweek,* May 13, 2002.

Richard Lowry, "Profiles in Cowardice: How to Deal with the Terrorist Threat—and How Not To," *National Review,* January 28, 2002.

Paul McMasters, "Blurring the Line Between Publicist and Journalist," *Neiman Reports,* Summer 2003.

Norman Mineta, "Facing the Tests of History," *Executive Speeches,* December 2001.

Victor S. Navasky, "Profiled in Cowardice," *Nation,* November 5, 2001.

Laura Parker, Kevin Johnson, and Toni Locy, "Secure Often Means Secret," *USA Today,* May 16, 2002.

Dennis Pluchinsky, "They Heard It All Here, and That's the Trouble," *Washington Post,* June 16, 2002.

Sasha Polakow-Suransky, "Flying While Brown," *American Prospect,* November 19, 2001.

Richard Posner, "Security Versus Civil Liberties," *Atlantic Monthly,* December 2001.

Thomas F. Powers, "Can We Be Secure and Free?" *Public Interest,* Spring 2003.

Anthony D. Romero, "In Defense of Liberty: Accountability and Responsiveness to Civil Liberties," *Vital Speeches of the Day,* January 1, 2002.

Jeffrey Rosen, "Security Check—How to Stop Big Brother," *New Republic,* December 16, 2002.

William Safire, "You Are a Suspect," *New York Times,* November 14, 2002.

Cam Simpson, "Latest Terror Suspects Seen as New Candidates for Military

Tribunals," *Knight Ridder/Tribune News Service,* March 18, 2003.

Solveig Singleton, "Symposium: Q: Will the Government's Use of Biometrics Endanger American Civil Liberties? No: Authoritarianism Is Not a Gadget, It's a State of Mind," *Insight on the News,* February 25, 2002.

Bruce Tucker Smith, "Symposium. Q: Are U.S. Military Tribunals Appropriate for Dealing with Suspected Terrorists? Yes: Such Tribunals Will Ensure That the Dictates of Both Fairness and National Security Are Met," *Insight on the News,* January 28, 2002.

Alisa Solomon, "The Big Chill," *Nation,* June 2, 2003.

Gene Stephens, "Can We Be Safe and Free?" *USA Today,* January 2003.

Geoffrey R. Stone, "Civil Liberties at Risk Again: A U.S. Tradition," *Chicago Tribune,* February 16, 2003.

Randall Stross, "Counterfeit Freedom," *U.S. News & World Report,* October 8, 2001.

Stuart Taylor Jr., "How Civil-Liberty Hysteria May Endanger Us All," *National Journal,* February 22, 2003.

———, "Military Tribunals Need Not Be Kangaroo Courts," *Atlantic Monthly,* December 4, 2001.

———, "Rights, Liberties, and Security: Recalibrating the Balance After September 11," *Brookings Review,* Winter 2003.

Laurence H. Tribe, "We Can Strike a Balance on Civil Liberties," *Wall Street Journal,* September 27, 2001.

Libby Tucker, "Gotcha!" *Science World,* March 7, 2003.

Bruce Watson, "Crackdown! When Bombs Terrorized America, the Attorney General Launched the 'Palmer Raids,'" *Smithsonian,* February 2002.

Fareed Zakaria, "Freedom vs. Security: Delicate Balance," *Newsweek,* July 8, 2002.

Jason Zengerle, "Infinite Justice—Can Courts Try Terrorists?" *New Republic,* November 19, 2001.

Internet Sources

American Civil Liberties Union, *Civil Liberties After 9/11: The ACLU Defends Freedom.* www.aclu.org.

———, "The Four Problems with Public Video Surveillance," May 22, 2003. www.aclu.org.

———, *Insatiable Appetite: The Government's Demand for New and Unnecessary Powers After September 11,* April 2002. www.aclu.org.

———, "Interested Persons Memo on Military Tribunals in Terrorism Cases," November 29, 2001. www.aclu.org.

———, "Interested Persons Memo on the Indefinite Detention Without Charge of American Citizens as 'Enemy Combatants,'" September 13, 2002. www.aclu.org.

———, "Q & A on Face-Recognition," September 2, 2003. www.aclu.org.

———, "Q & A on the Pentagon's 'Total Information Awareness' Program," April 20, 2003. www.aclu.org.

———, "Section 215 FAQ," October 24, 2002. www.aclu.org.

———, *The USA PATRIOT ACT and Government Actions That Threaten Our Civil Liberties.* www.aclu.org.

John Ashcroft, press conference, October 18, 2001. www.usdoj.gov.

———, "Securing Our Liberty: How America Is Winning the War on Terror," speech before the American Enterprise Institute, August 19, 2003. www.aei.org.

Joseph Atick, "Surveillance Technology: Tracking Terrorists and Protecting Public Places," *IEEE Spectrum Online,* October 31, 2001. www.spectrum. ieee.org.

Brooke Shelby Briggs, "Speak No Evil," *MotherJones.com,* October 4, 2001. www.motherjones.com.

George W. Bush, "Address to a Joint Session of Congress and the American People," September 20, 2001. www.white house.gov.

———, remarks at the Islamic Center of Washington, D.C., September 17, 2001. www.whitehouse.gov.

———, speech before the FBI Academy, Quantico, Virginia, September 10, 2003. www.whitehouse.gov.

Center for Constitutional Rights, *The State of Civil Liberties: One Year Later: Erosion of Civil Liberties in the Post 9/11 Era.* Center for Constitutional Rights, September 2002. www.ccr-ny.org.

Nancy Chang, *The USA Patriot Act: What's So Patriotic About Trampling the Bill of Rights?* Center for Constitutional Rights, November 2001. www.ccr-ny.org.

Muzaffer A. Chishti et al., *America's Challenge: Domestic Security, Civil Liberties, and National Unity After September 11.* Washington, DC: Migration Policy Institute, 2003. www.migrationpolicy.org.

Clyde Wayne Crews Jr., "Human Bar Code," November 1, 2002. www.cato.org.

Department of Justice Office of the Inspector General, "Department of Justice Inspector General Issues Report on Treatment of Aliens Held on Immigration Charges in Connection with the Investigation of the September 11 Terrorist Attacks," June 2, 2003. www.usdoj.gov.

Digital History, "Interpreting Primary Sources: World War I." www.digital history.uh.edu.

Marti Dinerstein, "IDs for Illegals: The 'Matricula Consular' Advances Mexico's Immigration Agenda," January 2003. www.cis.org.

Electronic Privacy Information Center, "Your Papers, Please: From the State Drivers License to a National Identification System," February 2002. www.epic.org.

First Amendment Center, *State of the First Amendment 2002,* 2002. www.first amendmentcenter.org.

John Fund, "Willful Ignorance," *Opinion Journal.com,* May 22, 2002. www.opinion journal.com.

James Glassman, "Time for a National ID Card?" November 4, 2001. www.aei.org.

Lawyers Committee for Human Rights, "Assessing the New Normal: Liberty and Security for the Post–September 11 United States," September 2003. www.lchr.org.

———, "Imbalance of Powers: How Changes to U.S. Law & Policy Since 9/11 Erode Human Rights and Civil Liberties," September 2002–March 2003. www.lchr.org.

Robert Levy, "Assaults on Liberty," Cato Institute, November 24, 2002. www.cato. org.

Dahlia Lithwick and Julia Turner, "A Guide to the Patriot Act, Part 4," *Slate.com,* September 11, 2003. http://slate.msn.com.

Paul McMasters, "The More We Know, the More Secure We Are," December 7, 2001, www.firstamendmentcenter.org.

———, "The War on Journalism," October 22, 2001, www.firstamendmentcenter.org.

Brendan Miniter, "Truth and Justice," *OpinionJournal.com*, August 26, 2002. www.opinionjournal.com.

National Immigration Forum, "Immigrants in the Crosshairs: The Quiet Backlash Against America's Immigrants and Refugees," *National Immigration Forum Backgrounder,* December 16, 2002. www.immigrationforum.org.

NOW: With Bill Moyers website, "Civil Liberties After 9/11: Timeline." www.pbs.org.

Ken Paulson, "A Matter of Balance: Secrecy Doesn't Guarantee Security," March 24, 2002. www.firstamendmentcenter.org.

———, "A Patriotic Press Is a Vigilant One," September 23, 2001. www.freedom forum.org.

Preserving Life & Liberty, "Stories and Articles." www.lifeandliberty.gov.

Mark Reibling, "Uncuff the FBI," *Opinion Journal.com,* June 4, 2002. www.opinion journal.com.

Ciro Scotti, "Politically Incorrect Is Downright American," *Business Week Online,* September 26, 2001. www.business week.com.

Phillip Taylor, "Summary of the Right to Privacy." www.freedomforum.org.

Jay Winik, "Security Before Liberty: Today's Curbs on Freedom Are Nothing Compared with Earlier Wars," *Opinion Journal.com,* October 23, 2001. www.opinion journal.com.

Index

Picture Credits

About the Author

James D. Torr is a freelance writer and editor who has worked on a variety of publications for Greenhaven Press and Lucent Books.